DISCOVER YOUR DREAM CAREER

Using Passion, Creativity, Thoughtleading and Fun to Attain a Worklife You Really Want

Ken Lizotte CMC

Copyright © 2014 by Ken Lizotte CMC. All rights reserved.
Published by emerson books, Concord Massachusetts, USA,
www.thoughtleading.com

Except as permitted under the United States Copyright Act of 1976, no portion of this publication may be reproduced or distributed in any form or by any means, nor stored in a database or retrieval system, without permission from the author or publisher. However, excerpts taken for review purposes or cited with appropriate attribution (title and author) in a book, article, blog etc., for the purpose of advancing an argument or message, ARE allowed within the guidelines of US Fair Use standards. Any use outside such parameters however will be considered an act of piracy.

NOTE OF DISCLAIMER: This publication is designed to provide accurate and authoritative information as regards the subject matter covered in its pages but is sold with the understanding that the publisher is NOT engaged in rendering legal, accounting or other professional services beyond the scope of this book's focus. If legal advice or similar "beyond-scope" expert assistance is required, the services of a competent professional practitioner should be located and retained. For further guidance, see the Resources page at the end of this book.

COVER GRAPHIC: WHAT DO YOU SEE? What we actually SEE when we look at the world is up to us. Do you see a glass half empty or half full? Do you view a sudden change in your life as a crisis or an opportunity? Do you immediately identify this book's cover graphic as a question mark within a circle or a swan spreading its wings to take flight or—if you turn the book upside down—a seal balancing a ball on its nose?
IOW … what do YOU see? It's all up to you.

ISBN: 0984718524
ISBN 13: 9780984718528
Library of Congress Control Number: 2014918143
LCCN Imprint Name: emerson consulting group inc., Concord MA

DEDICATION & ACKNOWLEDGMENTS

Writing a book in many ways is *not* a solitary endeavor. There is moral support from family and friends to whom you have revealed your ambition, and there will be editors and proofreaders and designers and other professional help along the way who cause you the author to re-think, re-frame, re-imagine, re-work and re-make what may have started out as an author's seemingly clear vision of his/her book but ultimately ended as a much different and, interestingly, clearer picture for everyone else.

So my gratitude for helping me see this particular vision through goes out first to Michaela St. Onge, my "deputy imaginative officer" at the time, to whom I first shared my plan to write this book, and whose response was an immediate, "Good plan!" It's taken a while to follow through since then but hers was the first encouragement as I started down the road.

Next come designer/techie Cindy Murphy and Elena Petricone (my current deputy imaginative officer), travel partners with me over the wildly arcane foreign soil of self-publishing. Even after many adventures and lessons learned there, we still haven't entirely mapped it out but we keep trying. One thing for sure, *that's* an endeavor one should never attempt alone!

Next comes my brilliant daughter Chloe with whom I shared relevant pieces of this book whenever she was wrestling with a career issue of some kind and who always, always, always returned the favor with a positive review, as in "I can't wait to read this book!" For a young writer as gifted as she is, that's double praise, from a target reader and talented writer all in one.

Next come the hundreds of CareerScapers who bravely took part in our "dream career" programs and went on to change their lives as a result. So many stand out as career heroes I literally cannot name them all here. But memories of some cry out for special attention especially those who volunteered to help with the programs so that a next round of participants could get the gift they had gotten, i.e., a new lease on their own career lives. Thanks then to Pat Cronin, Bill Hawkins, Ruth Pinkus (client #1), Sherry B. True, Bob Richard, Patrick Wheeler, Don Swavely, Carolyn Najarian, Bernadette Masur, Bob Moore, Rick DeAngelo, Dan Dangler, Bob Mendes, Diane Krause, Dave Mullaney, Areta Masi, Patrick Wheeler, Andy Karl, June Nagai, Jody Sharpe, Stefan Pagacik, Jim Pouliopoulos, Donna Linderman … a special but not exhaustive list.

Finally, CareerScape and its concepts, as outlined and explained in this book, would never, ever have developed into the shape it took by me alone. Without my business and life partner and wife of 20-plus years by my side, none of this would have grown from the germ of an idea in our two heads to a force of reality that, over the ensuing decade, altered the career behavior and mindset of so many, many individuals who sorely needed new hopes, new dreams, new personal and worklife victories. Her unmatched caring, energy, warmth, fun, left braininess, sensitive coaching, practical counsel and magnetic smile rallied every CareerScape room.

So to you Barb, light of my entire life, this book is dedicated.

TESTIMONIALS

Whether you're still in school, looking for work, or stuck in a job that is simply not satisfying, *Discover Your Dream Career* is perfectly designed to guide you to a career and a life that will be deeply satisfying and hugely rewarding. This book is rich with advice that will help you find the career path that is absolutely right for you. I know intuitively that what you discover in this very special book will redefine your life from ordinary to amazing!
     Lynn A. Robinson, author of *Divine Intuition* and *Trust Your Gut*

Are you ready to embrace your passion in life, your work and have a ton of fun along the way? No matter where you are in your life or career there is something for everyone packed in this toolbox of a book. Young, old and everyone in between, it is never too late to fulfill your dreams. I promise there is no other book like it out there in the market today. This book is your partner on your journey to the career and life you are searching for!
     Sherry B True, Owner & Service Provider at Spirit Paws, and CareerScape graduate

Having sponsored Ken Lizotte several times as a speaker at my WIND networking sessions, I can attest that he always delivers insights that my career explorer participants can use to succeed. His book offers similar tactical value, focusing on what kind of work a job seeker *wants* to find and how to find it, a 1-2 punch that can't be beat.

Fred Nothnagel, Executive Director, WIND (Wednesday Is Networking Day) and private career coach/consultant

Ken Lizotte's *Discover Your Dream Career* is a complete career workshop in type, with a host of real-life stories and dozens of thought-provoking exercises to get you off the couch and running toward your next great opportunity!

Doug Hardy, coauthor with Jeff Taylor of *Monster Careers: How to Land the Job of Your Life*

NOTE: For more testimonials, see this book's dedicated page on Amazon.

TABLE OF CONTENTS

Foreword..ix
When All Else Fails... 3
Prologue... 5
Chapter 1:   Your Personal Career Trap...................... 9
Chapter 2:   External Forces, Internal barriers............. 21
Chapter 3:   The Fear-of-Failure Gang....................... 37
Chapter 4:   What's Unique About *You?*..................... 61
Chapter 5:   What Can You Contribute? 83
Chapter 6:   Positioning Yourself for New Success 107
Chapter 7:   Career Treasure Chest 133
Chapter 8:   Moving On Up 163
Chapter 9:   How Social Media Can Help (and Hurt) 189
Chapter 10:   Settling Into New Digs 199
Chapter 11:   Thoughtleading for Career Success 217
Chapter 12:   Upon Graduating from College 227
Chapter 13:   Retirement Is Not an Option.................... 237
Chapter 14:   Balancing Work and Personal 243
Epilogue.. 259
About the Author and CareerScape....................... 263
About emerson consulting group inc. 265
Resources 267

FOREWORD

"What do you want?"

I spent a lot of time sitting at Ken Lizotte's conference table. Ken was my career coach many years ago when he started his company, CareerScape. At the time, I was an engineer working in a job I disliked for a company that didn't inspire me. I read an article in the local newspaper about Ken's career coaching services and decided to give it a try.

"What do you want?"

We met weekly at Ken's office. His conference table was usually strewn with paper, markers, scissors and other tools I used to complete the worksheets and assessments. I filled a huge three ring binder with pages of written exercises and hand drawn mind maps. Each week was an adventure in self-discovery and planning. I had never spent so much time thinking about what I truly wanted out of my career and my life.

"What do you want?"

I investigated and experimented with a variety of career paths. I met with countless people for career conversations. I slowly began to realize that my past experiences, education and skills were not necessarily a prologue of my future. They were just assets I could use or discard if they fit my picture of a dream career.

"What do you want?"

It was during one of the final verbal exercises that I had my most illuminating breakthrough. Ken sat in front of me and quietly but persistently asked me one question over and over again...

"What do you want?"

As I answered the question repeatedly, my responses began to change. My answers became briefer, clearer and, ultimately, truer. By the end of the session, I found myself answering that question with a simple, direct response:

"I want to help people. I want to teach."

After all the months of working on my dream career, I had distilled my vision to that statement. I slowly re-invented myself. I moved from engineering into sales and marketing where I could spend more time working directly with people and ideas. I went back to school and got my MBA to give myself a broader set of knowledge. Most importantly, I started teaching at local colleges as an adjunct instructor.

I taught college courses on a part-time basis for years while I worked in a corporate environment during the day.

Ultimately, my corporate jobs were never enough to feed my soul. The work was often uninspiring and the environment was too bureaucratic for my taste. When the economy crashed, I was laid off with thousands of my co-workers. I felt free.

I decided not to burn my bridges. I was professional and exited the company on good terms. However, I decided to burn my boats. I vowed never to work for a large, corporate entity ever again. I did not create a new resume. I did not go on job interviews.

FOREWORD

I decided to follow my dream career path. Today, I am a full-time faculty member at one of the best business schools in the country. I am also an executive coach who works with business leaders to help them find clarity, balance and increased effectiveness. I've never worked harder in my life but I've also never been happier in my career. And, I'm a better father, husband and friend having found my place in the world.

This book is a virtual version of Ken's conference table. Find some quiet time. Sit down and read it. Do the exercises. Something powerful happens when you think and write and draw. You'll gain your own clarity of purpose, your resistance to change will fade and you will find yourself filled with a newfound optimism.

"What do you want?"

Go find out.

Jim Pouliopoulos
Director, Professional Sales Program
Marketing Lecturer
Bentley University
Waltham, MA

EXPECT **NOTHING**

ACHIEVE **MUCH**

ENJOY **EVERYTHING**

WHEN ALL ELSE FAILS...

Long before "Mad Men," Barbara had set her sights on advertising as a possible career, spending many months and efforts during the height of a recession to land face-to-face meetings with prominent ad execs in Boston and New York. Yet none of these meetings ever led to an actual job offer.

One day she'd had enough. Her forays were always so careful, so polite, so professional, so deferential. It was time to step outside the box and try something truly creative.

So, reaching back to her roots as an English major, she sat down one day and thumbed through her Shakespeare college textbook, searching for a pithy quote to fit the situation. She was soon typing out a brief note to a top exec at Hill Holiday, the substance of which went like this:

> Dear Ms. Maguire,
>
> *"I am not yet of Percy's mind, the Hotspur of the North; he that kills me some six or seven dozen of Scots at a breakfast, washes his hands and says to his wife, 'Fie upon this quiet life: I want work!'"*
> —William Shakespeare, Henry IV, Part I, II, iv

DISCOVER **YOUR DREAM** CAREER

A good account executive might have helped. Work. It's that simple. Not much has changed.

Sincerely,

Barbara A Litwak

This go-for-broke Hail Mary pass opened the curtain. The next day, her phone rang, Hill Holiday calling. At the subsequent meeting, she was, for the first time, offered a real opportunity.

PROLOGUE

Something's been grumbling inside you for a long time. It's not your stomach (hey, you just ate!), so you're hard-pressed to know exactly what's going on. Yet each day that goes by, especially each workday or school day or job search, its impact on you becomes harder to deny. This grumbling, this gnawing ache has been gathering steam for a while now, and you've tried everything you can think of to relieve it.

"Maybe I just need a vacation," you said to yourself once upon a time. Then you took off on a great one, flew to the Virgin Islands, lolled about on the beaches, went scuba diving, consumed many fabulous meals, while the sun set over the brilliant turquoise Caribbean waters—and still that grumbling throbbed inside you the whole time. Ten days later you returned to your desk, cubicle, truck, briefcase or school dormitory seemingly refreshed. But the ache, within a day or so, came roaring back.

So lately you've been gazing in wonder at your colleagues around you, at the office or your school or with your support group, thinking, "What's wrong with me?" Everyone else around you appears so contented. They all seem very positive and even happy. They come in every morning so chipper, go about their work, finish up their projects, head on home. No apparent problems. Why can't *you* feel like that?

DISCOVER **YOUR DREAM** CAREER

How's Your Career Health?

Excuse me for a moment: May I play doctor now? I'd like to examine your "career health," if you don't mind; see if there's medicine to prescribe. I'll do my best to come up with an accurate diagnosis. Would you mind filling out a few insurance forms before we get started?

Seriously, if you've been flirting with any of the disgruntled feelings described here, take heart: You're normal! What's more, you know all those "contented" colleagues you see around you, those peaceful working folk you wish you could be a little more like? Well, guess what? You're probably more like them than you realize. Why, I wouldn't be a bit surprised if they all felt exactly the way you do. They probably think *you're* the most tranquil, contented colleague they've ever known!

Everyone experiences dissatisfaction about their work from time to time, or wonders where their first job will come from after graduation or in the midst of a job search. Often that really does mean that a good vacation is indeed what's called for. A little breathing space, a change of scenery. Sometimes that's really all it is. Once you've satisfied an urge to temporarily get away, your life and work tend to turn around, revert to normal.

Other times, though, it's more than that. When a "grumbling" keeps nagging at you, day after day, month after month, year after year, then things have gotten serious. If you stay in your present situation and deny this inner ache, you risk mental, physical, and emotional ill health. Left to themselves, unsettling conditions in our career lives rarely improve.

We can explore this further by giving you that checkup. Please answer each of the following questions as honestly as possible. Since they're all very general, just check off a response that seems closest to the truth. Your doctor (me) will return in a minute.

PROLOGUE

NOTE: If you are now a fulltime student, think of your chosen major as your career and imagine how you might respond. If you have been unemployed for a number of years, e.g., at-home mom or dad raising a family, consider your at-home activities and/or volunteer work as your current career.

	Yes	No
Have you been sleeping well?	_____	_____
Does your work challenge you?	_____	_____
Do you enjoy the people you work with?	_____	_____
Do you make enough money?	_____	_____
Do you feel well treated by your boss?	_____	_____
Can you identify genuine advancement opportunities where you work?	_____	_____
Do you find your work meaningful?	_____	_____
Would you like to be in this job five years from now?	_____	_____
Do you feel you are growing as a person as a result of your current job?	_____	_____
Do you look forward to going to work in the mornings?	_____	_____

DISCOVER **YOUR DREAM** CAREER

Do you look forward to Monday mornings?   _____   _____

Do you feel that your best talents are being utilized?   _____   _____

Do you feel that you're listened to at work?   _____   _____

Do you feel that you're given sufficient credit for the good things you do at this job?   _____   _____

How did you do? Did you check more yeses or more noes? If you checked more noes, I'll have to level with you: You've contracted a serious case of "wrong career disease." Yes, that's correct—you're not well.

But serious career illness can't be cured with vacations, weekends, a slight change in work assignments, or a dose of aspirin or penicillin. You're telling yourself with all these noes—let's say five or more—that you've just got to move on. Moving on to what, of course, may be the $64 trillion question. But move on you must.

1

YOUR PERSONAL CAREER TRAP

It's easy to step into a "career trap" of your own making. Such a trap has been carefully conceived and set in place by society over a long, long period of time. As such, it can be difficult to spot in your path and thus hard to avoid. You may have innocently set your foot inside it at one time or another and then grimaced as its clamps slammed shut. Clang!

What exactly is a career trap? It's simply when the great work that you have been doing, or that you do now or have been studying towards, rarely (or never) gets acknowledged as valuable work. Because even worse, someone may have once remarked to you, "*Anybody* could do it or learn to do it. It's really nothing special or unique." Translation: And neither are you!

But respect *is* a necessity for each one of us, especially if you're planning to turn yourself inside out and make a major career move. And seeing yourself as a unique and valuable contributor to the overall workworld is a requisite for maintaining respect for yourself. Otherwise, you begin believing that (a) you don't deserve a fabulous career life, and (b) the knowledge and expertise and individualized thinking that you've developed over the years aren't all that special. You then start devaluing yourself and disbelieving you can ever make such a fulfilling career move at all. And that buys you a one-way ticket to No-fun Land.

Help Is on the Way

Fortunately, by picking up this book, you've made yourself an important career commitment. You've actually decided to take command of your worklife. Whether you've been fantasizing about getting promoted, moving laterally to a new department, changing your career, quitting your present job, moving into your first real professional job after graduation—whatever! Something inside you has begun suggesting to you that you can do it.

So let's now gauge your level of positive thinking and self-confidence. If you've been allowing too many internal barriers to stand in your way, you'll need to start knocking them aside so you can ramp things up. For example, do you tend to yield too much power to external forces? Delay personal career victory by living off excuses? Put yourself continually in the background while others get the spotlight and pull it away from *you*?

In the worksheet below, answer the questions using the scale. Then we'll score your answers for a readout of your "positive self-belief"—that is, your level of self-confidence about your chances for genuine career fulfillment.

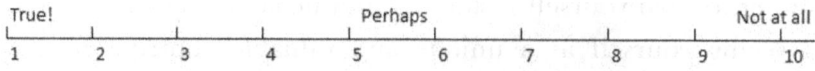

YOUR PERSONAL CAREER TRAP

1. Dreaming of a better life will get you nowhere. _____

2. You CAN fight City Hall. _____

3. Television is a vast wasteland. _____

4. Chances of finding a job I will enjoy are very unlikely. _____

5. There are no decent movies around anymore. _____

6. I'm not really a creative person. _____

7. Lending money to friends usually ends in trouble. _____

8. Cops are never around when you need them. _____

9. People do not understand me. _____

10. The world is my oyster! _____

    Total _____

Scoring:

    Give yourself two points if you marked an 8 or higher on questions 1, 3, 4, 5, 6, 7, 8, and 9, one point if you marked a 4, 5, 6, or 7 on these questions and zero points if you marked a 3 or lower. Then give yourself two points if you marked a 3 or lower on questions 2 and 10, one point if you marked a 4, 5, 6, or 7 on these questions and no points if you marked an 8 or higher.

Now total all your scores.

How did you do? Did you score 20? If so, you scored *big*! That's a perfect score, and it means you absolutely, no-question-about-it, couldn't be more of a positive thinker if you tried. You're optimistic, you believe in your ability to effect change, and you've got your barriers in check or you're constantly working on them. It's unlikely that you let yourself feel victimized for any great length of time.

NOTE OF CAUTION: Does this mean that you never have to work on your barriers, that everything comes easy to you? Probably not. More likely you have to work on your internal barriers the same as everyone else. But you probably give yourself effective inner signals to make your efforts at eradicating your barriers pay off. You've decided in your head that you can do it.

If you scored 15 to 19, you're on your way to career nirvana, although you're not quite there yet. You probably know that you've got to keep watch on yourself so you don't stray from the path. I suggest periodically asking yourself such questions as:

Which internal barriers do I most want to get rid of?

Which give me the most trouble?

What solutions can I think of to keep them in check?

YOUR PERSONAL CAREER TRAP

A score of 8 to 14 means you have some work to do. There may be a bug in your ear that keeps whispering something to this effect: "No matter what you do, you will probably never make it. Face it: there's too much going against you. It's just not in the cards."

So for you low scorers, it's time to set free that wild, never-say-die, high-flying bird that lives deep inside you.... and is crying to get out! Flick away all the naysaying that keeps getting in your way. Put this book down for a moment and begin flapping those powerful, elegant freedom-loving wings.

Go ahead now, do what I say, I'll wait. *Flap, flap, flap.*

Now, ahem, didn't that feel just wonderful? Practice such wing-flapping each and every day from now on. Practice at work, at your desk at home, at school. At Starbucks, in your car, at the gym, or waiting at a bus stop, getting cash from an ATM or Googling in the school library. Alone or in front of friends. Or strangers. It will make you stronger.

Did I leave anybody out in the scoring? Oh, you say you scored *less* than 8? Well, then, ahhh... you've got a *lot* of work to do! You have a few hills to climb.

But fear not; you won't be going it alone. After all... you did buy this book!

Trust me when I tell you this, and this goes for everyone: You've got greatness inside of you and you're about to display it. You're now embarking on a grand adventure that will take you to a new place, a happy and brave new world, at which you will discover your dream career!

DISCOVER **YOUR DREAM** CAREER

Before we go on however, let's define our terms. When I use the phrase "discover your dream career," I mean what I say. I have indeed lived and learned, I've been around the block (a few times, actually) and I, like you, graduated from the school of hard knocks. Enough clichés for ya?

All of which means that I am not recommending you discover your "fantasy career." Fantasies are just that: far-out yet deep in our minds, separate from reality, something that seems like great fun and excitement but in truth probably would not be so in real life. Fantasies ignore the downside of things and the pitfalls and the tough challenges. Fantasies represent perfection... which life is not.

So a dream is different, a dream is "a wish your heart makes," or so the theme song to the "The Wonderful World of Disney" used to insist many decades ago. Walt Disney himself, no slouch in his own life when it came to making dreams "come true," once uttered, "If you can dream it, you can do it." And many of us who have jumped over high hurdles to leap up lofty goals would agree with that: The first step is to imagine a seemingly impossible goal, i.e., to dream or wish. Next take a few steps toward making that dream/wish inside your mind more concrete, typically through such actions as writing it down, and/or talking it out with someone, and/or declaring it verbally to the world, and/or doing some research to gauge its practicality, and so forth.

You get the picture, right? It's about taking baby steps at first, sticking your toe in the water, trying this and that. OK there I go with the cliché bit again.

YOUR PERSONAL CAREER TRAP

In this book, we'll also meet quite a few folks who followed this very path and not only discovered a dream career but have lived to tell about how they eventually created their own. Your dream career is more than attainable, countless others before you have managed to attain their own and with the help of this book and your determination, you will too!

Legion of Career Heroes

NANCY HALE: Simply by Chatting

For more than twenty years, Nancy Hale had felt completely secure in her career. A high school history teacher, she'd been appointed head of the department at age 22, an event that would set the tone of her work and life for two decades. She could ignore recessions and job market turmoil and just go to work and do her job. As a divorced single mother, she could raise her son, Tim, and not worry about the outside world.

But after she passed age 40, Nancy's life changed. The cutbacks and layoffs and downsizings she'd been dimly hearing about, stories of work and family lives getting torn apart in private industry throughout the 1980s, suddenly came slashing her way. Her town's school board began chopping up its budget and eliminating entire departments. Once sacred cows, these departments had now been rendered obsolete, untenable, a luxury. She got word about her own dismissal from the newspapers: Her safe, secured, comfortable, familiar routine would be over at the end of June.

"I have no connections, I'm too old, I'm not qualified for anything else," she told anyone who would listen. She felt her life beginning to unravel. "I only know teaching. What will I do? What? I'm just terrified!"

Nancy worried about other blocks, too, great, lurking internal ones. As she considered moving herself from here to there, she confronted a truth about herself.

"I'm a classic self-saboteur," she confided to me. "Whenever I try to change my life I make sure I don't succeed. I'll do everything I'm supposed to, everything people say you've got to do to make progress, but I keep resisting the process all the way. I refuse to let myself succeed."

In the midst of this crisis Nancy surprised herself. With our guidance, she began by "de-whelming" herself, breaking down the scary big picture she faced, downsizing it into small, realizable steps. That got her started. With each step she advanced a little further down the path. And each time she stepped off, she automatically left an old place and arrived somewhere new: new vistas, new resources, and fresh possibilities.

By taking such beginning steps, Nancy got herself into gear, despite her terror. What form did her steps take? She simply began chatting with people. That was all at first, just chatting folks up. Here's my story, sad but true. Everyone she met got an earful: grocers, mailmen, gas station attendants, old friends. Astonishingly, the mere act of reporting her personal crisis to others released many of her blocks. People returned positive feedback to her about all her concerns.

"I'm trying to find out what I want to do next, but I'm not sure what that is," she told anyone and everyone who would listen. "I'm looking for a new opportunity." Nancy's openings were short, sweet, and candid. Now lob the ball back.

Nearly all the people Nancy talked to had some kind of idea, suggestion, or tale of their own life turnarounds to offer her. Many truly great conversations ensued, including not a few invaluable ideas from totally unexpected sources. Soon she had so many options to explore there was no time left for panic, self-denigration, or hopelessness. She could make this change, whatever it was going to be. She really could.

All these interactions, all this chit-chat with a purpose, propelled Nancy Hale into a new image of herself and of what life could be. She put all the pieces together, including her home life with her son, Tim. She could spend more time with him, help him grow, pay attention. She could feel more creative and confident and personally powerful than she'd ever felt working at the school.

Someone somewhere told her about a man who wanted to sell a profitable home-based newsletter. After speaking with others who ran similar businesses, Nancy quickly came to understand, to her amazement, how eminently qualified she was: Her excellent organizing and editing skills would enable her to set up the business easily in her own home, and she also began noticing a knack for coming up with creative ideas for better marketing the business. The ideas just started flowing through her head and she couldn't stop them. The more she thought of herself in this new role, in fact, the more she felt that she could manage this business even better than its present owner!

So she took out a second mortgage on her home, negotiated a fair price for all, and bought herself a new world.

"I'm independent now, in control of my life," she could later report to all those willing contacts and resources she'd met along the way. "Now no one can fire me, I'm running my own show. That forces me to be more creative, energized and alive than I ever was at the school! It's up to *me* to keep making things happen now. That's still a scary thought at times, but not so scary as the idea that I couldn't make my life work out the way I want to."

As so often transpires when people break through blocks and start taking command of their lives, Nancy's universe turned around completely as a result of her decisions. In the midst of all this remarkable personal change, in fact, her school reinstated her department and offered her old job back. Immediately she thought, "How dare they! They just got me used to the idea that they don't want me anymore, and I finally came to accept that. Now they want to drag me back. The arrogance!" How the lady had changed!

But Nancy reframed the dilemma as a window of opportunity, a challenge to her new assertiveness. What if she could shape this into something that worked for her? Sure, I'll come back, she decided to tell the school principal, but first I want you to release my accumulated retirement funds to me, then hire me on a part-time basis only, and at hours of my own choosing. The old Nancy would never have even thought of demanding all of this.

So Nancy Hale now works mornings as a teacher, the profession she carefully crafted throughout most of her adult life, and the rest of her day as a successful desktop publisher. She spends much time with her son, takes classes in areas of other interest, and runs her own life.

Do blocks and old doubts still rumble around in her head, taunting her, pushing at her? Sure, they keep trying to creep back in, she acknowledges, but they're no longer welcome, nor do they visit for very long. Whatever blocks come her way now, whatever terrors spring forward, she faces them down. She's worked out her own definition of balance, and she's made it reality.

2

EXTERNAL FORCES, INTERNAL BARRIERS

There's a scene in the movie *Working Girl* in which the Melanie Griffith character, Tess, as she begins her metamorphosis from admin to executive, tells her best friend and fellow admin about a networking function she'll be attending that night for upper managers. Looking over outfits, she holds up a shimmering black dress, calling it "simple and elegant."

"But it needs some bows or something," her friend says, snapping the gum in her mouth.

But Tess explains that she needs a dress like that because she wants to be "interacting with people not as a secretary but as a—"

Her friend cuts her off. "As a total impostor," she says, matter-of-factly.

Tess, a little stunned, stops for a moment, suddenly aware that her admin friend does not understand.

The sad reality of the career lives of many professionals and recent graduates, whether administrative assistants or otherwise, is that such internal barriers hold them back all the time. While the smart professionals take for granted that the level they're currently operating on only marks a staging area for their leap up to the next plateau, still others convince themselves, without questioning their assumption, that they've reached their limit.

Positive-thinking sales professionals, for example, know that if they work hard they may move up to sales manager, district sales manager, and perhaps VP of sales. Similarly positive engineers assume the opportunity to rise to senior engineer status, or to some specialized area of expertise, or to project management.

Another option for anyone might be to break off from employee status altogether and make lots more money as an independent consultant or by starting or running your own business. But where can the professional who feels stuck go, especially if they translate that feeling into an illusion that they are powerless to move up or ahead? Nowhere, that's where.

Yet although you, no matter what your current field or age or status, do have many external forces working against you, understand that people move out of their sticky, yucky world each and every day. I do realize it's not all you, that there are external forces too holding you back. But knowing that others before you have faced the same conditions and, despite them, affected great changes in their lives, may very well help you to do the same.

Fighting Your External Forces

In order to prevent these dreadful external forces from holding you down, we'll need to examine them. As we do this I'll also note a thing or two that you can do about them. Throughout this book you'll encounter many ideas for battling external forces.

Let's take a look at a few external forces now...

Subtle Signals in the Air

Just as Tess gets the message that trying to be other than an admin amounts to false pretenses, you too may hear or sense similar messages. You'll often catch these signals from bosses, higher-ups, customers, fellow students or colleagues. You may even get them from friends, or family. The first rule, then, is to refuse to let external forces set your agenda for you.

In *Working Girl*, Tess has plenty of subtle signals going against her, not only the self-trapping admonitions of her best friend but also the patronizing comments and treacherous actions of her conniving boss, Kathryn (Sigourney Weaver), a boss who absolutely cannot be trusted.

But she pushes her way through anyway, setting up her own plan of action and carrying it out methodically. Given the requirements of Hollywood, of course, her plan has to go awry, explode, and involve Harrison Ford. Still, she comes through it all with a very happy ending. But the moral of the story is that it is *possible* for an admin (or anyone) with sufficient spunk to dramatically change her life.

Not-So-Subtle Signals in the Air

Do you work for a company that sets strict criteria for its new hires and transfers? Maybe you're employed by a large bank, for example, that refuses to consider anyone without at least an MBA for any entry-level position, or by an academic institution that hires only professionals with a Ph.D?

Maybe you work for a company with a clear and obvious "career track." Once you're on it, you'll be considered for a higher-level position in the same vein as your current position, but there's no chance of anything more or anything different. Personnel discourages you, your boss discourages you, managers in other departments don't want to risk "stealing" you away. Direct official barriers to your advancement make it all feel so hopeless.

Throughout this book I'll touch on many ideas for breaking through such barriers. But for the moment, let me leave you with two.

1. Why not go back to school for a master's degree or MBA? Or Ph.D? Well, why not? As you listen to yourself protest and dredge up excuses, think of this: People (not you yet of course) do it all the time.
2. Just because a thing has never been done before doesn't mean it can't be done. People who blaze new trails are called "pioneers." You could be one too.

Say your company has never moved anyone that you know of into a new career area. Why couldn't you be the first? You'd obviously have to devise a creative strategy and work real hard at lobbying the right people. You'd have to prepare yourself for a different kind of job interview than what you've been used to. But so what?

Think of yourself as today's version of Lewis and/or Clark, Amelia Earhart, a young Tom Edison, a middle-aged Priscilla Alden! Why not *you*?!

Bosses Who Won't Mentor

Everyone works overtime in today's business world. There's always so much to do that if you're not literally pulling down more than forty hours, you're nonetheless likely to be overtaxed mentally, physically, and

EXTERNAL FORCES, INTERNAL BARRIERS

emotionally in some other way. If you must survive a major layoff, downsizing, or restructuring, you'll undoubtedly end up with more to do than you ever had before. For the forward-thinking professional, this development represents both good news and bad news.

The good news is that in the midst of great change you might possibly encounter more opportunities to get involved with major projects and important decisions than might ever have been allowed before the cutbacks. With managers and project teams suddenly needing all the extra help and resources they can get, they may start relying on you to do a lot more than you have been doing so far. That means the chance to learn, grow, spend time in other departments, get to know higher-level professionals on an equal basis, and generally build a reputation as a valued player who can be called in to help in a variety of ways.

The downside of such a new order in the workworld, however, might be that your manager or supervisor could become so busy and distracted that she'll have less incentive than ever to spend time "developing" the staff. As a result, she may be relying on you more than ever to pull your heaviest load in terms of what you've been doing for the company for far too long. In her harried new frame of mind, the last thing she'll feel she needs is for a sensational, lifesaving pro like you to be even *thinking* about leaving for greener pastures. Thus your spectacular track record may make it harder and harder for you to get out than ever before. You might feel like you're digging your own grave.

What to do, what to do? Paul Falcone, a human resources expert who has written books on this subject, suggests that the answer may lie in making a mentor out of your boss. Only with your boss's support, Falcone feels, will the chances be good for you to make a move within your present company.

But … start your boss off slowly, considering her present stressed-out frame of mind. You might test the waters, Falcone says, by asking her to sign off on an outside training program, preferably on something that could extend your chances for advancement (say, a communications workshop or some public speaking or accounting).

"See how your boss reacts," he says. Since these programs are frequently quite inexpensive, you'll know that "if this seems too formidable a favor to ask, you've got your answer. It'll be time to look for a job elsewhere," i.e., outside the company. But if your boss does go for it, then you'll have begun to move her into a new frame of mind that will help you get what you want.

A more on-site idea is to volunteer for a special assignment, perhaps one that your boss needs to execute but either doesn't want to or doesn't have time for. Once you get the go-ahead, especially if your boss is willing to supervise you, you'll be home free. You'll both relieve your boss's stress and teach yourself a new set of skills. Any good manager will quickly see what a boon you're becoming. You'll have even saved him the trouble of doing the delegating!

Suppose you know, for example, that your boss needs to execute a cost-accounting project for one of your department's subdivisions. You know too that your boss hasn't exactly been looking forward to this project. Also, despite repeated (and valiant) attempts to find the time, she just hasn't been able to.

One day you walk in all bright and cheery-eyed and lay an action plan on her desk. Handing over an eye-catching, carefully detailed agenda, replete with timelines and clear objectives, you announce, "Here's how I'm suggesting we implement the cost accounting review for Triple-X

Division. I know it's been an impossible project for you to get to, so I'd like to help. If you'll just guide me and answer any questions I might have, I'll do all the calculating, computer inputs, and spreadsheet reviews. You keep checking on me from time to time and by the middle of next quarter, we'll have everything completed."

Woweezowee! This has got to be sweet, sweet music to your frazzled boss's ears. By virtue of *your* initiative, this vexatious task that just wouldn't go away is finally going to get done. Your suggestions will have expanded your job description *and* created a mentor for you in one fell swoop.

NOTE: Of course, moving into accounting may not be your thing. So substitute whatever kind of new career you might be thinking about. Then look for a similar project that you can tackle which will enable you to build your skills in that career… and get paid for such skills-development as well!

Structure of the Company and/or the Job

Sometimes the very structure of the job or the way a company may be set up can keep you stuck. In a larger company, for example, function may be so tightly organized that no one is allowed sufficient slack to transfer to a new department or to learn something new. Hiring is always done through search firms whose mandate is to find someone on the outside. That means middle managers, technical personnel, financial professionals—you name it! Even those in upper management feel trapped by the system. No one on any level ever gets the chance to make a move.

Smaller firms too, particularly the smallest ones, may be similarly inflexible. Though as a general rule small firms offer environments that require everyone to pitch in and help with everything, sometimes organizations with extremely specific job functions drive the work atmosphere the other way.

Janet Travis, now a sales executive with a major consumer products firm, recalls an eye-opening experience at a company she worked for in her early career. After many months of doing not much more than what she had been hired to do—mainly compile and review proposals and other formal documents—she expressed her frustration to her boss, the attorney who had hired her, about the lack of intellectual challenge. The job, she confided, was driving her nuts.

"I need to do something that allows me to be more creative," she said.

Her boss, however, minced no words. "I never hired you to be creative, I hired you to pore over documents. That's the job here, that's all it is, and that's all it can ever be."

His blunt response was motivating, Janet recalls now, laughing about it. "It motivated me to get the heck out of there! I immediately began taking steps to find a new job."

Internal barriers

Now let's examine more deeply those "internal barriers" we spoke of earlier, specifically those that block us, young or old, experienced or neophytes, from moving ahead in our careers. As much as we might like to foist all the blame for our lot on external forces, most of the responsibility for lingering in an unsatisfactory job will usually rest on our own two shoulders. We are only human, after all, suffering to one degree or another a myriad of neuroses, self-doubts, and lapses in self-esteem. Some of these afflictions are especially common to those in the lower

EXTERNAL FORCES, INTERNAL BARRIERS

ranks of the professional ladder, a victim of the external forces in their environments as well as symptomatic of the personality type that gets attracted to, and perpetuated by, this work.

Kind of makes your head spin, don't it? There's a lot of work to do, it seems, a lot of change that has to go on inside. Of course, we're not saying that all of the internal barriers mentioned here belong to *you*. You may personally be way ahead of the game with some of them. But others may be getting the best of you and, if that is so, it's critical that you know that.

By identifying your internal barriers, you'll contain and corral them, wrestle them into submission, maybe even set them loose to run away from you and hassle someone else. The main point to remember is that *you* are the boss here. You can do anything you want with your internal barriers—ship them off to a different department, make them sit in a corner without any lunch, hand them a pink slip. But what you've got to know first is what they look like.

Life Point Analysis

To identify your internal barriers, you place them within the context of your whole life. Your barriers typically surround themselves with your fears and anxieties about who you are, what you're capable of, what the world expects from you. They want to help you, they really do, and you should pay attention to what they're trying to say. But you should never let them hold the reins.

In the blank space below, draw a picture of yourself. Yes, you heard me right: *Draw* a picture of yourself. In fact, if you rummage about your house or office for some crayons or markers, you may end up having a lot of fun with this! C'mon, let's head back to childhood, when we never cared about self-esteem, insecurity, or fear of success or failure. We were having too much fun!

Don't read further until you've finished your self-portrait.

EXTERNAL FORCES, INTERNAL BARRIERS

I AM WAITING PATIENTLY FOR YOU ...

BUT PLEASE TAKE YOUR TIME!

Now that you've completed your self-portrait, go back and insert positive and negative "life points" that populate your life. Include talents, skills, dreams, and proud achievements as well as fears, anxieties, worries, and bad habits. Insert your positive and negative "life points" by drawing them all around your self-portrait. Do not use any numbers, letters, or words. (That's correct. You read me right again: no numbers, letters, or words—just drawings.)

Instead, just rely on your natural creativity and let yourself have some fun. When you have finished, resume reading.

I AM WAITING PATIENTLY FOR YOU ...

BUT PLEASE TAKE YOUR TIME!

Now, let's analyze what you've done. Contemplate these questions:

1. *What happened when I asked you to tackle this assignment?* Did you enthusiastically grab a box of markers or crayons and excitedly whip together your self-portrait? If so, that one step—picking up crayons or markers—something you did even before the official exercise began, showed a willingness in you to do whatever it takes to advance your career and personal growth. You trusted that trying something different might advance you a little bit further. You took a chance. Good going!

2. *What did you fret about either a bit or a lot in regard to a picture of yourself?* Did you think at once, "What, me draw? Oh I could never do that—I'd be laughed out of my house and village!"

If you felt even a tinge of this but went ahead anyway, you too showed the willingness to brave your fears. You took a risk despite an inner barrier that tried to stop you. Jolly good show, old sport!

3. How'd you do on the next part, adding in your "life points"? Did you struggle at times to find a way to depict good and bad points without using numbers, letters, or words? If you did, but you struggled bravely through anyway, please know this: Whatever you put on the page, no matter how it looks, has demonstrated your innate ability to be creative. It doesn't matter at all what it looks like, either (so tell your cat to stop laughing). You simply devised a way to communicate something in a new way. That, my friend, is what in the business we call creativity.

4. On the flip side, did you get down on yourself because you couldn't think of a way to pictorialize every point? Did you worry you might not have executed this exercise perfectly? If so, please be warned: Perfectionism is an occupational hazard in the business and workworld. It's a characteristic or "skill" that will typically get us in trouble.

So let your perfectionism dribble away. You can't move forward if you demand so much of yourself, it bogs you down. Instead, you'll only stress yourself out and hesitate to take a needed next step.

And you've *got* to take such next steps, they're your life-giving career actions that will catapult you from your current state into a brand, spanking new and desirable one. Thus don't feel you need to do everything perfectly. Just go out and do it well.

EXTERNAL FORCES, INTERNAL BARRIERS

Legion of Career Heroes

BOB RICHARD: Risking It All

When Bob Richard got laid off after twelve years as a test developer with a government personnel division, the incident turned him into a self-described basket case. At 43, he wondered where else he might work, what else he might do. He was utterly shaken.

Sensing the need for a support structure to get him through what he foresaw as a potentially painful transition, he decided to join a job search support group. Such an action was a major one for Bob because he'd always studiously avoided groups of any kind. He'd always been scared of them.

"I'd just never been comfortable in a group," he said. "I never enjoyed the atmosphere of groups, or the dynamics, or the participation required. People always seemed to take to groups more naturally than I ever did. It made me tremendously self-conscious. I can't explain why I felt this way, but I always had, all my life, and I'd never been able to shake it."

This time, Bob was willing to risk all because he could imagine the benefits. The danger from trying to wing his way through a period of unemployment, at a time when there was so much competition around, seemed a vastly greater risk.

As Bob began looking around for a group to join, he encountered a huge block almost immediately: He couldn't find one! Any group he located met too far from his home or met too infrequently. He realized one day with a major shudder that if he wanted to join a job search group at this point in his life, he'd have to stand up and start one himself!

Initially he figured he'd offer his living room one night a week to a handful of unemployed professionals. He'd sit quietly in the back and just serve the coffee.

> But the first night I was startled to find that, far from feeling anxious in my little group, I found myself enjoying it! It was amazing, thrilling! It was one of those rare moments when suddenly you learn something very new about yourself that you never knew before. I could enjoy taking part in a group. I was hooked.

He really was. Before long, Bob Richard found himself not only coordinating his own "little" group (which grew steadily until he had to move it out of his living room into a church hall) but also assisting other fledgling job search group leaders as they struggled to get their own groups started. Though he endured the usual "learning curve"- the normal mistakes and stumbles along the way that teach us new skills- eventually he graduated to running bigger and bigger groups and even founding and administering a statewide coalition of job search group facilitators.

As a result of all this experience, Bob was offered a position as a workshop leader and group facilitator with a quasi-governmental agency. Ultimately he became known to training professionals all across the state as "The Group Guy." Bob Richard had become a "groupie" in a big way. As he explains it:

> I've come to love the process of helping individuals learn from each other through a group format. When leading workshops in my current job, I find I can relate to people's feelings very well because I've often been through a similar struggle in my own life. I've had people break

EXTERNAL FORCES, INTERNAL BARRIERS

down crying in one of my groups over a personal problem, and I can instantly develop a rapport with them and foster the right group support. That helps them through it.

This kind of experience has added a new dimension to my life that has made me feel worthwhile. It affects my personal life too. When I'm preparing a workshop, my wife sees me walking around the house smiling to myself. That makes for a happier home life for everybody. I'm lucky to have found this.

3

THE FEAR-OF-FAILURE GANG

If our internal barriers showed up regularly on the TV program "America's Most Wanted," the one barrier that most Americans would *really* want to see captured—the kingpin of them all—would be Fear of Failure, also known by such aliases as Fear of Success and Fear of Fear Itself.

Like some horror monster gang boss, this barrier may be towering wickedly over all your others—it has a proclivity to do that!—paving the way for your other internal barriers to keep running amok and wreaking terror over you wherever and whenever they can. Perhaps that's why it can be so tough at times to accurately distinguish between Fear of Failure and Fear of Everything Else. Our failure fears are just that ginormous.

In my work over the years with career-minded professionals, Fear of Failure/Success invariably rears its nettlesome head sooner or later. CEO, executive assistant, editor, police officer, financial consultant, security guard, barista—it does not matter one whit who you are. Sooner or later, for better or for worse, you will eventually and ultimately find yourself up against your own personal version of the fear barrier.

In Jan Halper's book *Quiet Desperation: The Truth About Successful Men*, male CEOs discuss their innermost feelings about their successful climbs to the top. Surprisingly, Halper's results reveal tremendous levels of fear inside these men too as it relates to the very implications of their career successes.

Many CEOs worry, for example, about being able to continue their success and/or about greater responsibilities created by each new success and/or about what they would do if suddenly, somehow, they lost their job. Despite having proven their abilities again and again, these folks still have to shore up their confidence each and every day against their fears, anxieties and even terror (eye-eeeee-arghhhhhh!) of what failure and even success could bring.

So fear of failure/success is a universal problem, an ingredient we all manufacture within our psyches au natural which affords us the delightful propensity of plunging ourselves into too-deep waters by causing us to sometimes pay too much attention to it. By automatically giving it the power to dominate us, we allow it to tell us what to do.

"If I'm afraid," we reason, "I must not be doing things correctly." Yet often we know, way down deep, that we in fact *are* doing the right thing. What is going on, simply, is that we are simply feeling very scared. And since we do not *enjoy* that feeling we then try to get rid of it any way we can. So the easiest way (we reason erroneously) is to succumb to its wishes.

Ethel Cook, an independent consultant who started out as an executive admin, recalls a career experience that illustrates exactly what I mean:

THE FEAR-OF-FAILURE GANG

Once, as an admin, I had successfully put together an important conference of my company's major executives. My boss was so pleased with this work that he wanted to acknowledge me for it in front of all the attendees.

"Ethel, it's only right you get credit for what you've done here. This meeting wouldn't be taking place without you. I'm going to introduce you to everyone, and then I'd like you to say a few words. Just say hello and maybe thank everyone for coming—it doesn't have to be much. I just think you deserve a few moments in the sun."

Despite such a generous honor, I freaked out. "I won't do it," I cried. "I can't get up there in front of everyone and give a speech. I can't do it. I won't do it."

"No, no, not a speech, Ethel, just a few words. You don't have to say much, just 'Hello, thank you for coming,' then sit down."

Even so, I was still terrified. What if my voice gave out? What if people laughed at me? What if I ended up sounding like an idiot? I felt I just couldn't do this, that I wouldn't be able to successfully pull this off even for the briefest moment.

"No, I won't do it," I declared again, more vehemently than before. "And if you make me do it, I'll quit!" Ouch! My boss finally gave in. I was simply not going to stand up there in front of all of those people no matter what he said even at the cost of my job itself.

Deep within, Ethel knew she was surrendering to her fears, and thus losing something in the bargain. Intellectually, she knew she could, in fact, do this, and that she might even succeed at it. But her Fear of

Failure (in front of an *audience*, no less) had blinded her from taking this very necessary, if very scary, first step.

Ironically, as the years went by, Ethel started to develop a desire to leave admin work and become an independent consultant. She knew, however, that this work would require her to do lots and lots of public speaking. Yet with her fears still gripping her inside, she now began attending Toastmasters, a public-speaking club, and taking every opportunity she could to get up in front of audiences and brave her willies. She got actively involved with a national seminar company and also with the National Speakers Association, such that, years later, she began commanding "substantial fees" for giving talks or seminars. She admits today, too, that she still gets nervous before a presentation but these times she refuses to let her anxiety keep her down. Yes her fear monger still lives within, but no longer does it hold its ugly power over her and prevent her from attaining career success.

Anxiety and Fear as a Signal to Grow

Obviously, letting our fears run our lives rules out exciting opportunities for career advancement. Ethel might have embarked on her successful career as a consultant and speaker years earlier had she accepted her boss's invitation to just say hello and thank everyone. Of course all of us can look back on our lives, both professional and personal, and recall similar incidents when our fears held us back from doing something we knew would lead us forward.

Yet, when new opportunities arise, we sometimes fall into the same trap, i.e., a downward spiral we too easily slide into. To get out of this counterproductive mindset, we must practice substituting a different, healthier one. What if we saw failure, for example, as a learning experience? That's after all what it really is, an opportunity to discover how to do something at all, in order to understand precisely how to do it right, and well, and to our greatest advantage.

Susan Schenkel, in *Giving Away Success: Why Women Get Stuck and What to Do About It*, puts it like this:

> Since by definition a challenge isn't a sure thing and thus some failure is inevitable, such failure must be viewed as a temporary setback that creates an opportunity to learn. It becomes a cue to try something else, not a signal to withdraw. Sustained effort in the face of setbacks allows one to persist long enough to attain success. This in turn reinforces a more optimistic attitude toward future failures.

Schenkel should know what she's talking about. She has studied the subject for many years and taught courses on it at major universities. She has also observed the dynamics of failure-as-a-barrier and "sustained effort" as a method of breakthrough in the clients she sees in her psychology practice. I observed the same dynamics in my career exploration seminars and not just in women: men get easily stuck in this black hole of anxiety and fear too.

Take the case of Sam, an accountant working for a company based in Detroit, who told the following story at one of our CareerScape workshops:

An opportunity to travel to the company's Northwest branch and review their financial records had come up. Although qualified to represent his company on these service missions—he'd handled hundreds of departmental financial inquiries and problems over the years and knew the company's accounting procedures inside and out—Sam nonetheless immediately began thinking: "I'm afraid to ask for this assignment because I don't know what my boss Jim would say. Would he laugh in my face? Would he say I'm not capable of going out to another branch on my own, that I only know about headquarters finances and not those of a branch office? I just have no idea what Jim would say."

He knew his fears were ridiculous but they nonetheless grabbed hold of him. He was terrified to ask his boss Jim for the assignment.

So at first he gave in to his fears. "I just won't go ask him. It's better that I don't know what he thinks. Hearing negative thoughts about me would be devastating. Besides, what if he took a chance on me and I blew it?"

But after a few sleepless nights, he decided otherwise. "Forget it! Why am I so afraid I might blow it? Besides, if I don't even try new things, how can I ever grow or succeed? How can I move up to a higher rung? I have to ask for this even though I'm afraid of what could happen."

The next day, revving up his courage, Sam went to Jim's office to ask him about the assignment. At first Jim in fact did hem and haw a bit about Sam's going off to a branch office. "You've never done this before," he said. "How do I know you can handle it? Are you familiar enough with our branch offices' procedures?"

Braving his own self-doubts, Sam just rattled off whatever came to mind and within seconds heard himself telling Jim that he planned to call the branch's CFO for a briefing before he left for this trip. "I'm very good at picking out flaws and discrepancies even within procedures I'm not acquainted with," he said. "I often can solve problems that no one else on a team has even spotted. So I feel pretty confident I can get up to speed."

Was his voice wavering too much as he made his case, he wondered? Was he acting confident enough, was he successfully hiding his deepest anxieties? He didn't know for sure but he pressed on anyway. Then suddenly, as if he had heard enough, Jim pulled out a travel voucher and put Sam's name on it. "You're right," he said, nodding his head. "You've come a long way since that day you walked in here as a junior accountant. So let's get you on a nonstop flight to Seattle and let you do what we both know you're good at."

So rather than let his anxieties and fears stop him, Sam learned they could be signposts for growth. We often fear something because it represents something new and unfamiliar to us, fear of an unknown. It's a natural, important fear that gets our adrenalin pumping so that we are alert and ready for action. *Can I really do this?* We ask ourselves. *Am I up to the task?*

Then as we worry and think it through, we come to realize that we'll never know the answers to such questions unless we try. So we push through our fears, as Sam did, and ask for (or take) what we want.

This by the way is the key ingredient, i.e., breaking through all your fears, doubts, and anxieties and getting on with your life. Don't let your Fear of Failure (or Fear of Success) stymie your actions. Let fear help you examine an opportunity to see if it's right for you, to pique your sense about it. But never let your ultimate decision be based on Fear of Failure alone. Failure will happen and will help us learn, and so the fear of it must never be the sole criterion for moving ahead or remaining in one place.

Fear of Success

Regarding Fear of Success, what is it really but just a variation of Fear of Failure? Like those CEOs in the book *Quiet Desperation*, it's only a postponement of the inevitable. It reveals a deep-seated insecurity about one's intrinsic ability. Listen to a few statements from top professionals in their fields who were willing to share their deepest feelings about this subject in our career programs:

Sylvia, who runs a real estate firm in White Plains, New York: "When I succeed at doing a great job at a new project, I think: but won't that just postpone failure to a future date? When I succeed, I think I'm often just lucky, or that somebody's giving me a break. People simply haven't seen through me yet. So what's the point of succeeding? They'll just find out I'm incompetent later."

Tom, manager of a construction company in Denver, Colorado: "If I succeed, I might not like what I've succeeded at, and I'll be disappointed. If I get disappointed, there must be something wrong with my ability to make decisions. It'll highlight my poor sense of judgment, which I already feel I have. Why go through all that? Maybe I'd better just stay where I am and quit kidding myself."

John, owner of a retail chain in Vermont: "I always wonder if I really deserve to succeed even when I do. I'm always thinking, 'This isn't me, this isn't me.' You may think I'm a competent person, but I'm not as good as you believe I am. It's an intense doubt that's deep down inside me. It's a feeling that makes me want to get as far away as I can from any of my successes."

Can you see how Fear of Success feeds directly off Fear of Failure? "If I succeed, it'll either postpone failure or risk that people will find out I didn't deserve to succeed in the first place." That's the sum of what

THE FEAR-OF-FAILURE GANG

we sometimes think. Or this: "It'll show off my other failings, like poor judgment."

Golly willikers... you can't win for losing, can you?

Fear Breakers

Enough talk! Let's get down to putting some of our fears to bed. Or at least to identifying what we can do about them so they don't keep holding us back.

In the space below, list as many career fears as you can think of. You may list Fear of Failure, Fear of Success, Fear of Mediocrity ...*any* fears that come to mind. If we want to contain or eradicate our fears, we've got to get them clearly out into the open.

After you've listed all your fears, list an idea for braving each fear beside or under that fear. Don't worry about how confident you are about your idea working (that's only another example of your fear!). Just jot it down. As time goes by, you'll have the chance to try out your ideas and see which work and which don't. If an idea doesn't work, of course, you've still accomplished something: You'll have risked, and experienced, failure, but you won't have let it hold you back!

Most experts who study human fears, and professionals who have successfully prevented their fears from holding them back, tend to agree on one remedy: action! No matter how difficult, frightening, worrisome the fear, the best way to eradicate it or gain control over it is to do something with it or about it. In her excellent book *Feel the Fear and Do It Anyway*, Susan Jeffers offers a central message you might give yourself while initiating such actions: "Whatever comes as a result of facing my fears, I can handle it."

And she's right, you know. Our most basic fear is that we won't be able to handle whatever unknown or unpredictable result comes our way because of our actions. We don't believe we're capable of dealing with the ramifications of facing our fears on our own. Maybe our fear or anxiety is really an ancient primeval instinct alerting us to keep our senses clear, our heads up, and all our wits about us. "Do your best, your absolute best, with everything working at full capacity," might be another way of saying it.

But whatever you do, don't hang back and do nothing. You really can handle it.

Sam, for example, "handled" the momentary ambivalence expressed by his boss Jim by refusing to let it affect him. He felt his gravest fears rising anew as he wondered aloud about his own abilities. But he stuck to his plan, kept himself talking. He didn't stop, run, hide, or back down. He took action.

Ethel Cook, later in her career, finally stood up at a podium for the first time and risked all the laughter, ridicule, disapproval she'd feared for so many years. But it didn't materialize, and that only made her a little stronger and more confident to stand up at a podium a second time, then a third, and a fourth, and again and again. Over time, she became a seasoned professional speaker, still with fears, but this time in control of them.

The Helper Mentality: Special to Women

A charter member of the Fear of Failure Gang, the nefarious Helper Mentality makes its appearance throughout the world in many guises, all donned primarily by women. Female nurses, for example, are the helpers of both male doctors and other female nurses. Mostly female human resources professionals help out their mostly male division managers and CEOs in business.

Other professional helpers staffed mostly by women include therapists, social workers, counselors, customer service reps, admins and teachers. Anything primarily viewed as a "helping" role, it seems, will tend to draw most of its practitioners from the ranks of females.

Janice LaRouche, author (with Regina Ryan) of *Janice LaRouche's Strategies for Women at Work*, labels this phenomenon "The Helpmate Block." In her comprehensive exploration of internal barriers that directly affect professional women, LaRouche explains:

> Playing the traditional helpmate is a hard habit to break. Not only is it ingrained in us as the truly feminine way to be, but it is also part of a deal: I help you become successful, and you take the ultimate responsibility for my welfare.
>
> Many women, instead of focusing on what they can get out of the workplace, typically spend much of their energy looking for opportunities to give. Yet seeing themselves in this way—as givers, not takers; as helpers, not leaders—stops women from figuring out the real needs of a situation and how best to respond.

It stops them from taking initiative and accepting responsibility. And it prevents them from doing what's best for themselves and for their own careers.

Only by giving up this support role, LaRouche insists, can women helpers truly learn to support themselves. That's because the mere act of letting go of the compulsion to support others (to the exclusion of one's own needs) puts an end to concurrent overreliance on others for support. She suggests that when we stop caring "too much" about others and expecting others to care "too much" about us, we begin filling up our caring gap by focusing attention and support on ourselves.

Women professionals thus should heed LaRouche's advice. It's an occupational hazard, like perfectionism: You spend every minute of your workday toiling to assist someone else (or a crew of someone elses), leaving precious little time or energy to think too much about yourself. It's a bottomless pit.

In some ways, of course, there's nothing new about this. Back in what we might call the Age of Loyalty, when job security was in flower, workers knew that by doing their jobs the best they knew how they would be rewarded, promoted, and, at the very least, kept working ad infinitum by their employers. Little time or attention need be accorded to extracurricular career development. You took care of someone else (your boss, especially), and he took care of you. That simple.

Sometime during the 1980s, however, the music died and the Age of Loyalty came to an end. Now no female helper can merely perform her helping job and take for granted it'll still be there even a week from now. This goes for men too. We've all now got to have a plan now that job security is dead. We've all got to help, and keep helping, our own selves.

Self-Support Mind Map

One way to help you speed this process along might be through a Self-Support Mind Map. But what the heck is a mind map, you inquire? Well, it's a creativity technique for exploring an issue by opening it up to the artistic corners of your brain. It's a nonlinear, daydreamish approach that takes the perspective of problems-as-discovery. It also lets you examine an issue over time by allowing for ongoing inputs and ideas.

You can construct your own Self-Support Mind Map by scrawling the words *How I Support Me* in the center of a sheet of poster paper (or two or more 8 ½ by 11 sheets of paper taped together). Using markers or crayons, map out—via tentacles or wavy lines—key characteristics, vexing problems, goals, potential solutions, next steps, and supportive resources.

At the end of each line or tentacle, you might write categories such as "Career Desires," "Personal Life," "Educational Interests," "Actions I Must Take," "People Who Can Help *Me*," "Resources I Can Call On" etc. Then you draw pictures along each line and/or shoot off secondary lines/tentacles from the main lines to denote subpoints and side issues.

For example, subpoints of "Educational Interests" might include "Finishing my degree," "Taking relevant workshops," "Reading more books." You'll then make notes to yourself around these points, such as "Call colleges for course catalogs," "Go to library and scan computer section," or "Check with adult-ed center for relevant workshops." Some of these elements, or subpoints, might connect naturally with each other or with your primary categories (say, "Reading more books" with "Career Desires"). If so, run a dotted line between the two to show the connection.

To make the whole thing truly colorful and fun, paste in magazine excerpts, photos, quotes, and cartoons. Attach relevant objects if they'll fit: a ribbon, a button, a fortune from your fortune cookie. In short, convert your mind map into a lively collage of your thinking and imagination. Let it grow and deepen and interact until you have the fullest, most vibrant understanding of how to actively support yourself in your quest to successfully advance your career.

To keep your exploration of this issue alive, take a look at your mind map every day and keep adding to it or changing it or crossing off items you have achieved. Tape it on your bedroom or office wall, where you can easily see it. As time goes on, your Self-Support Mind Map will evolve organically, as will your ideas and resolve about achieving your goals.

Achievement Deficiency

What are you proud of? What accomplishments in your life do you recall enthusiastically? Can you immediately come up with two or three good ones? How about twenty or thirty good ones?

Or does your mind instead go blank when we ask such questions? If it does, you're undoubtedly a victim of another certified member of the Fear of Failure Gang: Achievement Deficiency.

Many folks display a notorious, almost gleeful, capacity to discount their abilities and achievements. Such individuals tend to assume that anything they've done can be chalked up to luck, or to someone else's help, or that a task they've performed or a talent they've exhibited is really nothing special. In *Giving Away Success*, Susan Schenkel cites this all too common inner barrier as particularly ingrained in women.

THE FEAR-OF-FAILURE GANG

"There are many ways we discount ourselves," she writes, adding, "When women are successful, it must be explained in some other way." Schenkel calls this the "feminine discounting habit," depriving women of ongoing positive feedback. Missing out on such feedback, she says, "locks out information needed to make optimistic predictions," preventing confidence-building and the upgrading of "unrealistically low expectations."

Schenkel concludes that, to the extent women attribute success to luck, tasks "anyone can do," or other people's efforts, "we tell ourselves that we aren't in control of our environment." Hence, Achievement Deficiency, i.e., the notion that you've never really done anything special in your life … and probably never will. Achievement Deficiency thus declares: "I'm just not that good, special, or powerful."

Young girls in particular have been taught to heed this sign. While boys may be encouraged to scale a wall, girls will be advised to not even try. After all, they might get hurt, fall, fail, or—God forbid—get dirty!!

I recall distinctly a curriculum track in my high school years (some years ago!) that the administration called "commercial course." Other school systems at the time may have labeled this track "business course" or even "secretarial program" but one thing was certain: boys rarely enrolled in this curriculum. Instead, boys who truly dreamed of getting involved in business took classes in "the college curriculum" and went on to higher education. Commercial, business, and secretarial programs were for girls only.

Much of this has changed since those heady, male-dominated days, but not all of it. Even today way too many girls and young women move on from their educational experiences believing they can only contribute so much in the workplace. Even those young women who understand the counter-productivity of such thinking nonetheless limit themselves by playing down their accomplishments. Somewhere along the way they learned it just wasn't feminine or at least that they themselves weren't all that special. Thus, their actions tend to reinforce an internal minimizing of their self-esteem.

Of Note to Boys and Men

Though women often harbor these limiting thoughts and deeds in greater numbers, I know many male readers may be thinking, "Yeah, but I sometimes (or frequently) feel exactly the same way."

For men, it may have come about as a result of similar misconceptions of how the world (and life) really works. Like women, men compare themselves to others, especially to other men (or boys when younger) who seem to be superior. Sports has always been one monumental example of a judgment system in which the frail or shy boy gets shunted aside to dwell within the shadow of the star athlete, say a clever quarterback in football or talented pitcher or long ball hitter in baseball. As a boy grows up, he may discover other, non-athletic talents and be rewarded for them and as a result this shucks off his self-conscious coil. Think nerds and geeks a la Steve Wozniak, Steve Jobs or Bill Gates… enough said?

Yet a part of this masculine inferiority complex may remain and do damage to said individual by holding him back from trying very hard to prove himself not only in the workplace but in life in general. So for the male gender as well, Achievement Deficiency can deliver its own brand of horrors.

Achievement Roll Call

But behold, fair reader, be assured there is indeed hope!

One way to get this particular member of the Fear of Failure Gang off your back is to dig down deep into the reality of your own genuine

THE FEAR-OF-FAILURE GANG

life achievements—by thinking about them, writing them down, reflecting on them and certifying they are true. It's too easy to forget that you really did do these things... *you really did!* So let's start by lining up a few up of them for inspection and paying them some heed.

In the space below, list at least five professional achievements. If you can think of more, use the margins for more space and list them too. Beside or below each achievement, note the reasons you feel good about what you achieved. When you have finished composing this list, read on.

How did you do? Did you complete the list? If you didn't, go back and complete it now. Yes, yes, you have indeed achieved at least a few great things over the course of your career, haven't you? Go back *now*... that's an order, corporal!

Looking at Your List

OK so *NOW* how did you do? I bet you surprised yourself the second time around. Maybe you came up with more achievements than you ever thought you would before you got started.

And what were the reasons that caused you to choose each achievement? In other words, why were you proud of whatever you listed? Next consider what your reasons say about you, and about the kind of person you are, and about your capabilities?

Your completed list will paint a picture of a very powerful human being. Your completed list is a display of your capacity to accomplish whatever you set your mind to. Consider: can you remember how you felt before you set your sights on one or more achievements? Perhaps you were scared, anxious, self-doubting? Yet you pushed through these inner (and outer) barriers anyway. You faced down your fears and made it through.

Well, guess what? You can do all that again!

Most folks find this assignment daunting at first. But maybe you didn't, maybe instead you just enjoyed it and mustered your enthusiasm for it and then completed it relatively quickly. If so, score a big fat A-plus for yourself!

On the other hand, if you struggled with the list but pushed yourself through to completion anyway, well, hey there: you get a big fat A-plus too!

If however you didn't complete the list, it's time for you … to … try it again, treat it as one of those challenges that can end up being labeled an achievement. Look, between you and me, just us chickens, we both *know* you can do this, right? I mean, we both *know* so.

So just go back over to the worksheet and finish up. Trust me, trust me… it's all going to be fine. We'll leave your A-plus waiting for you here on the edge of my desk. Please pick it up when you've completed your list.

THE FEAR-OF-FAILURE GANG

Recording your achievements and taking note of the personal abilities you employ to make things happen can enable you to keep your personal power in full view. Whenever you find yourself doubting your talent and potential, just whip this list out and take a good, long look at it. Each time you do, you'll undoubtedly have a few new achievements to add to the list. So do so!

By regularly renewing your understanding of how capable you are, you'll also renew and reinvigorate your confidence toward attaining your career (and life) dreams.

The Overwhelm Factor

How do you like the title of this section? Doesn't *The Overwhelm Factor* sound like a good old movie from the 1970s or 1980s starring Michael Caine and Brenda Vaccaro? Or maybe updated today with Justin Timberlake and Jennifer Lawrence?

Let's tackle the "original" version: Michael Caine is a British agent dashing through the busy, rainy streets of London, pulling Brenda along with him as she tries to hold on to her broad-brimmed hat. Big Ben is tolling in the background, but they've got to get to Scotland Yard before the bomb goes off in Buckingham Palace. Get there too late, and it's curtains for the Queen, England, and for Her Majesty's Empire. . . . *The Overwhelm Factor,* a Miramax/United Artists release, coming this holiday season to Netflix or a cinema near you.

Well—surprise!—the Overwhelm Factor actually refers to yet another member of the Fear of Failure Gang, yet another inner barrier common to us all. And—double whammy!—we have a *real* motion picture in mind that will help describe the Overwhelm Factor: It's called *What About Bob?* and was quite popular a few years back.

DISCOVER **YOUR DREAM** CAREER

In this "screwball American comedy," as the ads like to say, Richard Dreyfuss plays a noted psychiatrist who has written a best-selling book called *Baby Steps*. He hopes the message of his book will help daffy, neurotic Bill Murray get his life together—so that Murray will leave Dreyfuss and his family, vacationing at a lake resort, alone!

But need I add that dealing with a Bill Murray character, Dreyfuss' hopes are, well, dashed. And that's all I'm going to tell you about the movie's plot.

Interestingly, back here in real life, I find the message of Dreyfuss' *Baby Steps* "book" very instructive. I think the movie's writers really had something there.

So your solution is simple: Take a few baby steps!

Many professionals freeze themselves in their tracks whenever an obstacle in their career path looms too large. Though we will often think nothing of taking on a large-scale, derring-do project if our bosses assign it, including staying up late until all hours and tunneling through miles of online files and paperwork, and inputting and spell-checking, googling till the cows come home etc., we'll *less* frequently take on the same challenges for just ourselves. Because that's when all our other fears kick in, hitting us when we're down, e.g., Fear of Failure, Fear of Success, Achievement Deficiency—they all re-rear their ugly heads!

So take a few baby steps. OK, one step forward, that's it, then stretch the other foot out in front of you, then put it down again. OK OK, goooood … verrrry good! Now you're getting the basic idea.

THE FEAR-OF-FAILURE GANG

When faced with a seemingly overwhelming project, break it down into stages, steps, tiny pieces, whatever. What may seem like one hell of an impossible task can actually get accomplished with a considerably lighter load of stress. You might not even know for sure where you're really going, or what the end of the road you're on will look like but one thing you probably do know: You can't stay where you are forever and still make much of anything change.

Remember this old Chinese wisdom chestnut: "The journey of a thousand miles begins with a single step." Each new step therefore brings you closer. Even a tiny little baby step.

Legion of Career Heroes
CARL ERIKSON: Forbidden Questions

The expression "bought the farm" is a positive one for Carl Erikson. Once a successful attorney and business manager, Erikson and his wife one day made a monumental decision. They simply quit city life, leaving professionalism and their urban home behind, and moved to Vermont. It was a bold decision, a scary one ("I've had my moments of abject terror," Erikson laughs now), but it was a vital one. For much of his adult life, Carl Erikson had longed to work with textiles.

"I gave up fifty years of a certain standard of values," reflects Carl, the father of three grown children. "It took some soul-searching to get to where I could make this decision. But I've come to know this is right for me, not just all right." Officially waving good-bye to a business-oriented lifestyle, a path so honored and so rewarded in our society, he moved.

Carl began working with textiles early in his adult life, initially as a hobby turned passion that took control of all his free time. For a long while, he could see no way to turn this passion into anything like a job with which he could support his family. People surely can't make a living at this, can they? Besides, Carl often worried, should a grown man be engaging in what historically has been a feminine pursuit?

Yet Carl's expertise with the loom, sewing machine, and needle continued to grow. Before long, he found himself churning out the most brilliant scarves, tapestries, cloths, and robes. His enthusiasm and excitement multiplied with his expertise. He began to ask two forbidden questions: Am I certain this path truly embraces my heart and soul? And would I be willing to give up my present success, built so carefully and solidly over the years, to do this?

THE FEAR-OF-FAILURE GANG

Joining one of our programs got Carl finally "talking to people who really do this." He also began taking classes to improve his skills, and sharing his techniques and hopes for the future with other artists. He gradually learned how to become better at his craft, how to reach a public that cared to see the work, and how to begin to make at least an artist's living. It was not going to be easy, but he began to realize that it was possible. He was knocking on the door and, in amazement, watching it slowly creak open.

These days, on warm mornings or afternoons, you can find Carl Erikson sitting on the front porch of his secluded farmhouse near Brattleboro working on his textile constructions. He displays his work in New England art galleries as he looks for that first sale. Two years after he made the move, he has not found it yet. To make ends meet, he works two part-time jobs, and his wife works, too. But there are no regrets. He's done the right thing, he declares:

"I left behind those judgments from the business world where you worship income, material benefits, 'success.' I've no plans any longer, no interest, no wish to go back. I couldn't imagine going back, really. The remarkable thing about my life now is that every day I'm finding out who I really am. And that I have to do this."

4

WHAT'S UNIQUE ABOUT *YOU*?

Imagine you are holding a mega-lottery ticket in your hand. Yes, I understand that you'd never *ever* buy a lottery ticket; that's just not your style. Unless of course it's a Powerball that has just reached $325 million (or more). Otherwise… it's not how you roll. I get it.

Yes, lotteries are such a long shot, no one ever really wins them, at least no one you've ever met. Certainly *you* could never win. I get it.

Even so—let's call it a whim—or a rare moment of insanity—let's suppose you did indeed purchase a lottery ticket earlier today and now find yourself looking hopefully (despite yourself!) toward this Friday's stupendous $18 million jackpot. Hey, the devil made you do it. Yes, yes. I get this too.

Now comes 7 PM on Friday night and time for the "Lottery Live!" TV "show," only 5 minutes long because drawing the winning number is the only point of this weekly broadcast.

Again, I recognize you'd never be caught dead watching this fleeting on-air homage to legalized gambling, but for some crazy reason tonight you are. (El Diablo again!) Actually, you hadn't even planned to watch but you were flipping channels and suddenly—bazinga!—there was the snappy opening lottery jingle and, oh yeah you almost forgot, there was that ticket you purchased back on Tuesday, it's right there on the coffee table in front of you. "Oh, what the heck," you think. "I bought the darned thing, didn't I? Why not see what comes up?"

A moment later, the lottery machine's Ping-Pong balls go flipping and flying about in their cages, and then begin dropping one by one into preset slots. The number 3 comes down first, then 4, then 3 again. You glance somewhat half-heartedly at your ticket. Hey, you never win anything, right? No never! Ha-ha, what fun.

But tonight you observe that your ticket's first number is a 3, and that its second number is a 4, and … ah … your third number is a THREE! Weird, you think, as you momentarily lose a breath.

So now your second three numbers are 5, 7, and 2. Surely there's no chance that . . . but the next ball on the screen drops… and it's a 5!

Your heart is beginning to beat a little faster now. The next ball spills down. Gasp. "Seven!" you exclaim to no one in the room. The ball slides into place. . . SEVEN!

Holy moneybags, Batman! What if the next number's a 2? What'd be the odds?

You are actually standing up now, holding that ticket for dear life and unable to breath a whiff. *This cannot be happening*, you gasp.

WHAT'S UNIQUE ABOUT YOU?

The last ball drops. "Two, two, two, me, me, me," you chant. "2, 2, 2, 2." You're more spiritual tonight than you've ever been in your whole life. "Please, God, please," you pray by screaming aloud. "Two, 2, two, 2, two!"

You're like some maniac up on the roof of Caesars Palace in Las Vegas as the ball slides into place. "C'mon ... TWO!" you scream, "2, 2, 2, 2, 2, 2, 2, 2, 2."

The ball comes to rest. It's ... a ... 2! Strangers can hear your roar all the way from your basement apartment in Queens to the Fiji Islands— "I *won*! I *won*!" – with that lottery ticket sticking tight to your clammy, shaking hand. *"18 million dollars! I'm rich!"*

DISCOVER **YOUR DREAM** CAREER

Question of the Hour:
Now What Would You Really DO If You Had All That Money?

OK so you won already. Yes, convince yourself this scenario actually happened. Then:

Start making a list of everything you would do in the first twenty minutes of such newfound abundance. Picture yourself right there in that precise moment, right there in front of your TV, right there staring ahead as the screen turns its attention to an old episode of "How I Met Your Mother."

What exactly do you feel you would want to do next, with all that money, or because of it? What kind of freedom would it offer you, what kinds of dreams could you fulfill? What money matters would you clear up first?

Write everything you can think of on the following lines:

1. _____
_____
_____
_____
_____

2. _____
_____
_____
_____

WHAT'S UNIQUE ABOUT YOU?

_____

3. _____

_____

_____

_____

_____

4. _____

_____

_____

_____

_____

5. _____

_____

_____

_____

_____

Our scene shifts now to the proverbial morning-after, merely seconds after you have come and gone from Lottery Headquarters. Your first million has been deposited electronically into your checking account. So *now* what do you do?

List below more things you might do with your winnings especially in the first year. Here and on the next page, complete your "life dreams" list. Money is no longer any barrier.

_____

_____

_____

_____

_____

_____

_____

_____

_____

Now then, have you listed *everything*? Have you gone through paying off all debts, buying houses and cars for yourself and your friends and family, squirreling a sizable sum away in the bank?

Have you purchased travel tickets, a membership at your favorite golf club, all the latest fashions, vitamins to your heart's content, books, flat screen TVs, much bling and many, many baubles? Maybe you have packed your kids off to the finest, most expensive universities, secured season tickets to the ballet and your favorite NFL team? Bought each of your nieces and nephews a pony *and* a pachyderm and one year's supply of organic kibbles and bits?

WHAT'S UNIQUE ABOUT YOU?

I said *everything!*

What to Do Today?

Once you've conjured up everything you could possibly imagine that your winnings could achieve for you, such that you just cannot imagine even one thing more, consider this:

It's a Wednesday morning. You've gotten up late as usual and slipped on your purple mink bathrobe and your gold lamé bed slippers. You've rung up one of your maids to hoof it to your upstairs dining room with yet another fantastic breakfast of your choosing. This time it's salmon soufflé and caviar jelly on toast imported from Amsterdam. Guava juice, flown in direct from Tahiti of course. Coffee delivered personally by Howard Schultz. Oh weary me... whatever do the simple folk do?

One hour later, as you're relaxing by your Olympic-size swimming pool (the indoor one, not the one out by your prize-winning rose garden) and this question flutters across your gold-plated brain: What am I going to do today?

By now, you're sick of exotic travel and 5-star hotels and your private jet. Been there, done that, and many times over. So travel's out.

Shopping? Please . . . such a bore. How many times can you amble through Harrods or survey new goods by Prada? Besides, by now, you've got everything.

Movies, theater, a sporting event? Done and done and done. Bo-ring.

Today you want to do something really different. You actually feel like *giving* something this time, not getting. You want to contribute to the world, take on a challenge. You want to ... oh, the horror ... do some *work!*

Yes, playing the idle rich kid no longer brings it for you. You can now do any kind of work you want, you can actually contribute to the world. So you wonder and wonder: What could that be? What do I *want* to do? Not what do I *have* to do but... what do I *want* to do?

Remember the sky's your limit because now you're filthy rich. Now all you've got to do is choose it and it's yours. And you can choose anything. For the first time in your life you don't have to choose something practical or out of desperation. Now you can choose to spend your time each day doing work you *want* to do. So choose, already!

In the space below, write down anything that comes to mind. Don't be shy and don't worry if it seems unrealistic or unattainable. Just play along with this, trust me. Anything that comes to your mind that you would love to do for work—anything—will be acceptable.

Write as much down as you can squeeze in. Then resume reading.

WHAT'S UNIQUE ABOUT YOU?

Regardless of what you wrote in the preceding space, go on now to these following five choices. Do them all, as they will help flesh out your dream career direction.

Choice 1. Owning a Company

In the space below, write down the names of five actual companies that you'd love to own. Or list five *types* of companies you might like to own—for example, a dirigible manufacturer, a corn-husking service, a magazine conglomerate, a gourmet coffee shop, a dress shop. Whatever comes to mind.

What companies or types of companies did you choose? Remember, you're the boss here. You can choose any kind of company and run it the way you like (within legal limits, of course). Think about why you chose the companies you did. What attracted you to each? Was it the company's product or service? Was it the way the company is run (working conditions, customer service)? Was it the industry the company is in?

In the space above, summarize the principal elements that attracted you to the companies you chose.

Choice 2. Going Back to School

Now consider going back to school. Remember, money is no object. In fact, you can't stop laughing when the admissions clerk asks if you'd like a financial aid application. Hardy-har-har! That's a good one, Norton!

In the space below, write down a list of courses you'd like to take, degrees you'd like to earn. If there are specific schools you might like to attend, jot the names of these schools down as well on the same line as the course or degree program. You'll get into any school you apply for, remember. You're what they call a "full-fare." Money talks.

What's most important here are the courses and the degree programs that you chose. They offer you clues to the type of work you might like to do next. So which courses, which degree programs? What exactly appeals to you about these courses? Do any relate to the companies you decided to buy? Is there any theme or pattern emerging? Which subjects did you choose that simply sound as if they'd be a lot of fun to study? Remember, you don't *need* to work, but you can if you want to. Since you wouldn't be doing it for the money, what kind of work would feel just like play?

WHAT'S UNIQUE ABOUT YOU?

Below, summarize the reasons you picked these particular schools and courses of study. Place heavy emphasis on why your chosen studies might be fun.

Choice 3. Contributing to a Cause

Now consider contributing heavily to a cause. Don't just throw your money around, though. Think about something you could really care about. What kind of a world would you like this to be? What societal problem would you like to solve? What suffering would you like to erase? What kind of boost would you like to give someone?

In the next blank space, list five causes you would contribute to. Place a figure for the amount of your contribution after the name of each cause or organization. Don't skimp, these are causes you truly care about.

And don't forget to sign the check!

So who gets the benefit of your largesse? What causes did you choose? Note that whatever you have decided here could have tremendous impact on the kind of work that you find meaningful. It could offer you a personal sense of contribution to the world through your worklife. Why should work simply be carrying out other people's orders, other people's missions and visions? What kind of world do *you* want? Why not implement your values through your work?

Below, summarize your thoughts about the kind of world you want to help create. How might you contribute to your vision through your own efforts? Don't worry about the ultimate realizableness of your vision. If you don't try, there's ZERO chance of succeeding. Do just think here about what matters to you.

Choice 4. Trading Places with Someone Else

Now how about trading places with someone else in the world of work? Rich dude or dudette like you can do this if you really want to, right? Just bribe somebody to let you take their place and perform their job for a while. (Everyone's got a price, right, Moneybags?)

WHAT'S UNIQUE ABOUT YOU?

So whom would you choose to trade places with if you could? Whom do you *envy* for the work they do? List five people you'd be excited to trade places with:

Whom did you choose? Was it people you know personally, or was it an individual you've observed from afar? What appeals to you about these other people's work? Why would having their skills and carrying out their line of work mean so much to you?

Summarize your feelings about these questions below.

Assessing Your Choices

Now review *all* responses. Look them over and note how they connect with each other, how they feed off each other, how they support each other, and even how they contradict each other.

If any do contradict each other, could this seeming contradiction be viewed in a positive light? How could your contradictions be complementary or combined?

Consider this example: Suppose you notice you're interested in farming. You love all aspects of it—cows, sheep, agriculture, the barns and tractors and farm implements. You also want to work indoors, however, in a nice cozy office setting, with quiet elevators and brassy door handles and lots of computers. How could you work on a farm and still go to work every day indoors?

Consider some ideas in the next blank space. Play around with your thoughts. Let your imagination run free. Any ideas are valid. Just consider what kind of options you can come up with that would accommodate both farming and working indoors.

Finished brainstorming? I bet you came up with some pretty wild (and yet feasible) ideas. Here are a few of ours:

- You could work for a government agency such as the Farm Bureau.
- You could work in the main headquarters of a large corporate farm.
- You could be a field inspector who visits farms from time to time but doesn't spend every day or all day on them.
- You could work in a farm museum.
- You could work for a farmers' lobbying group in Washington.

Get the way the game is played? At first glance, we don't always see how our seeming contradictions can be accommodated. But when we let our minds go free, they always can. Our imaginations can be awesomely powerful instruments. Use yours today.

"My Work Interests" Mind Map

About time for another mind map, wouldn't you say? With all these new themes, ideas, patterns, clues, directions running around in your head now, you've got to get a handle on them. What better way than a "My Work Interests" Mind Map?

Place the words "My Work Interests" in the center of a sheet of poster paper or two sheets of regular-size paper taped together. Run enough lines or tentacles or spokes out from the center to represent all of the categories I've had you review. Remember to spin off any subcategories or ideas for exploring each main category. Add lots of pictures and doodles and connect whatever needs to be connected with dotted lines.

You know the drill. This should really get you moving! From here on, it's going to be fun, fun, fun!

***

Intermission

Feel free now to get up, stretch, go out to the refrigerator, or take a walk outside. We'll resume our action in just a few minutes.

***

Hey there, everyone! Good to see you back so refreshed and revitalized. What did you come up with? As before, notice any themes that run through your mind map:

- What kind of work interests keep coming at you?
- What kind of conditions do you find you want to work under?
- What kind of people do you want to work with?
- Whom do you want to serve as customers or clients, and why?
- What kind of personal satisfaction will you reap from your work contributions?

Are you coming up with any crystal-clear answers yet? Is anything leaping out at you? If so, congratulations! You've begun to identify the kind of work you'd like to move toward. And you're way ahead of the game if you can do this now. Good for you!

If, however, your answers are still not quite so clear, do not fret or angst. We're not through yet discovering, not by a long shot. Maybe, though, you can discern a few clues. If so, tuck them away for future reference. Clues, as Sherlock or Matlock or Nancy Drew will attest, are what get us down the road toward a complete solution.

And yes, you will get there. Just keep collecting your clues and depositing them in your "My Work Interests" Mind Map. Your understanding of the work you want next will grow and grow. Don't give up the ship.

What's Unique About *You*?

So far, I've been guiding you toward answers that will help you know what new work you might *want* to do. We think that's the best place to start, in contrast to more traditional approaches that begin with what you have thus far demonstrated you *can* do. While it's valuable to be clear about what your skills are—they're certainly a component of the mix that defines who you are and what value you hold in the marketplace—such knowledge doesn't assist you all that much in moving to a new line of work. For that, you've got to know what *excites* you.

Your demonstrated skills at best represent only a small slice of the potential pie that is you. They don't speak to your capacity for learning new and different skills based on your talents and enthusiasm. Focusing only on skills merely traps you in a cage of limiting thinking.

That's why you must be cautious when your loved ones, friends, colleagues, even career advisers "wisely" caution you about the long odds of your breaking out of your workplace ghetto. They're only trying to help when they say things like:

"It's a tough job market out there."
"You've got to be crazy to leave a good job like this."

"All you're qualified to be is (fill in the blank)."
"You'd have to start at the bottom if you switched fields."
"Why would anyone hire *you* for a job like that?"
"Maybe you should just try for a little promotion."
"I wouldn't want to see you get hurt or disappointed."

It's nice of our friends and family to want to help us, but the problem is that such advice doesn't really help. For the most part it keeps us focused on what we've done in the past and not on what we might accomplish in the future. It speaks only to skills and not to potential or undeveloped talent. What they're not heeding is how frequently such molds get broken by motivated individuals and how strong our human spirit is to accomplish new things.

Though no records are kept on how many people try to change their careers and how many succeed or fail in the bargain, anecdotes abound that prove it can be done! And each tale of success points to the abundance of human talent waiting to be put in motion. You are indeed more than "just an admin" or "just an iron worker" or "just an attorney." Indeed, you are so much more.

Talents and Skills Unite!

So let's turn now to your talents as well as to your demonstrated skills. We want to look at the kind of work you *want* to do as well as how far you've come in showing that you *could* do it. Your skills, as I've just pointed out, tend to be focused upon first and foremost because they're visibly out there—they serve as living, breathing manifestations and advertisements of your capabilities.

Other talents may have shown their faces in your worklife as well, although sometimes a job doesn't let us show certain talents, which then lie quietly inside us, waiting for their big chance. Consequently, you've got to inventory talent too if we're going to define clearly all of what's unique about you.

Talents and skills must be seen not as a way to contain you but as expansive and versatile facets of yourself that are applicable to many, many situations and needs. Only our internal barriers prevent us from seeing where else our talents and skills can contribute. Our imaginations, in contrast, unlock closed doors.

Listen to a few reflections of successful former career changers who saw the light one day and recognized the transferability of their talents and skills:

Brittany: "I have excellent organizing skills. They served me well as an executive assistant, but now that I'm in account management they save me so much time. I look around at my co-workers and I see them late for appointments, forgetting to return phone calls, losing paperwork. Those kinds of things are the least of my worries. Instead, I get to concentrate on what really needs to be done—watching our client accounts and keeping clients happy!"

Jamie: "I was always good at greeting customers and making them feel comfortable when they visited my reception lobby. Now I do the same thing, as a customer service representative, and get paid a lot more for it. And I've earned such great performance reviews, I'm now being considered for manager of the department! Those days working the reception desk really paid off."

Patrick: "I was always poring over the company budget with my boss back when I was his assistant manager. For some reason, I had a knack for seeing details he didn't, and he used to acknowledge me for it. Now

I'm the company's corporate comptroller. Budgets here are more sophisticated than they were back in my department managerial days, but it's chiefly the same activity. I'm quite good at it too. Always have been."

Everyone struggles with the notion of "transferable skills" because it can be so hard to see ourselves objectively. Yet when we step back and observe what we've gotten acknowledged for, i.e., what we've often shown a "knack" for, that's when we begin to define our uniqueness.

"Only Me" Collage

Find or take a photo of yourself and paste it in the center of a sheet of poster-size paper. Make it one that's all smiles.

Now draw or paste around your photo symbols or pictures that characterize your talents and skills. Figure out what these are by analyzing your daily activities and by studying your professional achievements. What have you found that you are good at? What have you learned to do well? What functions do you perform, even those you don't feel particularly good at? What have you been praised for, rewarded for? What have you learned or accomplished that you never thought you could?

Note here any talents that don't get exercised much (or at all) in your work setting. Maybe these are things that you do well off the job. Maybe you just *think* you'd be good at them if given the chance. Look back at your list of people you envy for their jobs. Do they do things you think you could excel at, if given the chance? Paste or draw in these talents and skills.

Use cutouts from magazines or Internet sites to supplement your imagination. Complete this segment of your collage, then go on to my next instructions.

Enlisting Your Friends and Colleagues

Now let's get a few other brilliant minds into the act. Ask your friends to contribute to your collage. What do they see in you that perhaps you've missed? Are there talents and skills they've observed in you that you haven't depicted? Show them your collage and request inputs. Then paste in cutouts or draw in their ideas.

Next, do the same with colleagues. These are folks who *really* know how you operate on the job. You may be surprised at how supportive (and delighted) they'll be when you ask for their help. Choose only positive-minded colleagues, however. There's always a Debbie or Dickie Downer in every group who lives for the chance to drag you down into a dark, dank career pit. Stay away! You want this to stay fun.

Analyzing Your Results

Theoretically you could keep adding to and subtracting from your "Only Me" Collage for the rest of your life. It's a process that doesn't need to end. We are all, after all, ever-changing masterpieces that are continually growing, learning, achieving. So keep thinking up new things and enjoying how your collage shifts its shape.

For the moment, though, let's take stock. What's your first impression here? What kind of a picture have you painted of yourself? What skills and talents are confirmed in your collage? What's here that you hadn't expected to find? Do your talents and skills suggest a usefulness in any career areas that appeal to you? Do your talents and skills suggest career areas you'd never considered before?

In the blank space below, make a list of all skills and talents that have found their way into your collage. If you run out of room, keep going on separate sheets of paper. You want to have as clear a picture as you can of what's unique about you. While any one specific skill or talent won't be unique to you, the combination of all of them will be. In the next chapter, we'll investigate career areas you might want to pursue. Along the way, you'll be referring to this list and collage (which, remember, you can keep adding to). In doing so, you'll start pinpointing to what extent you presently display the specific skill set or talent set that this or that desirable career requires.

5

WHAT CAN YOU CONTRIBUTE?

It's easy to downplay how valuable we are. It's all too easy also to underrate the skills and the expertise that we bring to our jobs or that we've proven in college or in volunteer endeavors. We go about our workday each day, we get better and better at it yet we keep forgetting to recognize how much improvement takes place. The ease with which we perform our sometimes complicated, always sophisticated duties replaces our original maze of confusion, awkwardness, and uncertainty. No one compliments us about what we do and no one tells us that we're making progress. We just plod along to the beat of our own career drummer… and we get *better!*

For the moment, then, let's wax philosophic about the role you play. Have you ever thought, for example, about your work in "larger" terms? Have you ever acknowledged yourself for the indispensable contribution you make in your workplace, school, charitable or socio-political organization? Can you see how much less effective the whole operation would be without you—you personally—as a part of it?

Some of you probably get schizophrenic signals about how valuable you are. On the one hand, you're told, perhaps by your boss: "I could never afford to lose you," "You're my right arm," and "We could never have done it without you." On the other hand, should you come around asking for a raise, more time off, or greater responsibility, suddenly your boss pulls the wagons into a circle. "Well, ah, OK, but there's no money in the budget" or "Well, ah, one week off is the most I can give" or "Well, ah, you know a lot of folks would kill to have your job! It's tough out there." Shudders.

Small wonder then that most of you when caught in this situation throw up your hands at the mere mention of career advancement, resigning yourself to a five-day-a-week pressure cooker that you may *hate* for the rest of your natural working life. Contribution to society? Forget it, pal!

Scorning Retirement

If you want to advance yourself, you've got to hack your way through this demoralizing thicket of mixed messages and make your way to a clearing. What, in fact, do you *want* to contribute? What kind of legacy do you *want* to leave behind? Is there something about who you are and what you do for others that's especially meaningful to you?

To people who love their work, dreams of retirement never enter the picture. When people believe in what they do, when they feel that the world gains significant value from their career contributions, when they experience a continual sense of growth and positive stimulation, they scorn retirement. No longer doing what they do now at some point in their later lives suggests more stress than doing it forever.

The great vaudeville and 20th Century TV and film comedian George Burns, when he was age 94 in 1990, announced that he'd just signed a five-year contract with Caesars Palace in Las Vegas. "Imagine that," he

WHAT CAN YOU CONTRIBUTE?

mused, "me, a *five-year contract*." Pause, beat, customary puff on his cigar, then the punch line, "Normally I never sign a contract for less than ten!"

To his dying day of 100 years very young, George Burns never understood why anyone would retire. Certainly he refused to do it himself, playing Vegas and other venues right into his final year. George loved what he did, seeing the effect it made on his audiences nightly. He clearly understood and felt his contribution.

Whom do you know who thinks and acts like old George did? Celebrity heroes of yours, people in your own life? They keep on working and staying in the game, clearly impacting others. The evidence of this makes their work worth doing and their life worth living.

As an experiment, suppose you are heading for your retirement party. Let's imagine that you're being driven in a limo toward the big event all decked out in your finest threads and licking your lips at the thought of tonight's gorgeous feast and all those sparkling retirement gifts amassed on a special table. Hundreds of guests will be bustling about, eager to honor you.

It's going to be a swell time, you can bet on it. But then you settle back in your limousine and begin to wonder what speakers tonight will be saying about you. Oh, you know they'll have great things to recall about your days in both the trenches and the high spots. And they'll toast you and sing your praises to the rafters.

But *what* exactly will they say?

So you watch the trees outside glowing in the twilight as you begin thinking about that, and about what you'd *like* speakers tonight to say.

You start thinking about what you've tried to do in your life and the effect you've tried to have. You start thinking about what you achieved and how much good you have done. After a while, you've got it pretty well set in your mind. You know exactly how you'd like to be remembered.

How You'd Like to be Remembered

Here and on the next page, jot down a few tributes you'd like to hear about yourself during speeches at your retirement party tonight. Keep in mind my list of questions. Use the margins if you'd like to add more ideas.

1. What kind of an impact have you tried to have on people's lives?

_____

_____

_____

2. What specific contribution do you want to be remembered for?

_____

_____

_____

3. In what ways have you tried to improve the order of things?

_____

_____

_____

4. What value have you tried to add to the way things have always been?

_____

WHAT CAN YOU CONTRIBUTE?

___

5. What problems have you been able to solve?

___

The Arrival of "The Job"

Now that you've thought about your skills, talents, and contributions, it's time to consider constructing a "partnership." In today's workworld, the concept of partnership is actually an age-old concept insofar as it is considered an arrangement between individual entities of equal stature. It has, however, lain dormant throughout much of the past 30-40 years as corporate hierarchies developed and stratified the workworld. So many layers of corporate organization have all but dwarfed the worker bees inside, so it's easy to assume you have no power in your workplace whatsoever.

Yet viewing yourself as equal to whomever you might next work for (or with) is crucial to also seeing yourself as an individual whose uniqueness can maintain a powerful and continually marketable presence. In fact, in the good ole olden days (the *very* old olden days), true partnerships were quite common, and even assumed. Workers plied their trade with others of similar economic means and social position: farmer, tinsmith, blacksmith, weaver, whatever your station. The way it worked was that you ran your own business, sold your goods, offered services etc. to a variety of clientele in both town and countryside.

But you also purchased or traded goods and services with those who provided something you couldn't supply yourself. Though kings and lords dwelled hither and yon, for the most part people engaged in commerce in a spirit of equality within the same general economic class. Because most peoples' labor was so visible, so down-to-earth, they, of course, could also see clearly how their work contributed to the general welfare.

Then, somewhere along the way, the concept of a "J-O-B" arrived. This all started innocently enough—a little machine shop here, a crafts cooperative there, both of which needed "employees." Then, as the 19th century cranked into the 20th, a frenzy of workplaces got bigger and more powerful, demanding strong bodies to haul objects, fit pieces of things together, screw on bolts, work a new type of work mode called the "assembly line" ... and then repeat all these tasks over and over and over from morning till dusk, day after day.

People began to migrate, too. The predominant work model became a Monday-through-Friday (or Monday-to-Saturday), forty-plus-hours-per-week, fifty-weeks-per-year job slot, compensated with a "living wage" (in contrast with the old idea of a fee for services) and perhaps two weeks' "vacation" (something that used to be taken whenever one wanted, throughout the year). Some job slots even offered "benefits" such as health insurance, a retirement plan, a pension and life insurance.

What at first glance might have seemed progress, however, insidiously stole a great deal away. As individual workers were placed into narrow job slots, they suffered a disconnection from what their work really meant. They stopped experiencing the satisfaction of the customer at the end of the line, for example. In the auto industry particularly, a worker might drill a hole into one corner of a car's chassis for eight or nine hours each day, five and a half days a week, and fifty weeks a year. And this could go on year after year, decade after decade.

"What do you do?" the autoworker would be asked at a social gathering or on the street. Likely he'd have two potential responses: "I drill holes" or "I work for General Motors." But never: "I make cars." Because he didn't make cars, although he was a tiny part of the overall process. Nope, in this worker's own mind, he might see cars he had worked on driving down a road, but that end result was a far cry from the hole drilling duties he performed every day. He was thus a hole-driller, not a carmaker.

It's not surprising, then, that this disconnection would be felt by today's workers too. As various professions have gotten more and more specialized, many employees find themselves unsure of where they fit in, or what's the true impact of their day-to-day duties. When you're just doing a "job," that is, a series of tasks defined by someone else, rather than seeing a direct effect on an end result, you come to feel like a replaceable cog in a gigantic, incomprehensible machine. You feel as powerless as a bug. You certainly don't view yourself as an equal partner.

Partnerships to the Rescue

But there's a way out of this "disconnection dilemma." If you keep looking inside yourself, defining your skills, talents, and abilities *and* your passions and contributions, you can create partnerships in your worklife similar to those that existed before the Age of The Job. Once you do that, you'll be much more in touch with the meaning and impact of your contributions and thus you'll experience more genuine satisfaction from what you do.

In order to achieve this, you've got to now go beyond defining your own uniqueness into identifying who wants it or needs it. With whom can you partner to create a win-win economic exchange? Who has a problem that *you* can solve? How can you peddle your newly defined skills and talents so that each of you in this partnership wins, that is, so that you'll find yourself with work that's meaningful, challenging, lucrative, and enjoyable? Answering such questions ensures that your newfound partner will gain a service that advances his or her goals too.

You may have to break the bounds of convention to do this though, perhaps even the break with the way you've been brought up. Our parents and grandparents, after all, were by and large born and raised in the Age of The Job. They became acculturated to attitudes and behaviors associated with how to be a successful employee not a successful "partner." And that has drained down and drenched all of our culture. So many of us have got to learn new ways to think and act.

To help you condition, or recondition, yourself, consider the following statements made by professionals in today's world. Which seem in tune with the principles of work *partnerships*, and which with being a darn good *employee*? Record your answer by writing in your choice after each quotation.

Harriet: "I know what I'm supposed to do each day. That's one good thing about where I work. My boss always has it clearly laid out for me—packaging mail, upgrading the software, re-checking correspondence. He's extremely well organized."

Keith: "I'm constantly on the lookout for new projects, new things I can learn from. It doesn't take much extra effort to find them either. I just keep asking people, 'How can I help you?' … and they tell me!"

WHAT CAN YOU CONTRIBUTE?

Suzanne: "I've got this idea for a new way to greet company visitors. Instead of just having them sign in at the reception desk, we could hand them a company brochure and offer them coffee while they wait. We could spread goodwill and promote ourselves while we make them a little more comfortable. I've already suggested this to our operations manager."

Thomas: "I know I'm good at what I do. I work overtime, take work home, do personal errands for my boss. I go way beyond what's expected. So where are those two extra personal days I've seen other people on my level get? And why am I not being given more responsibility and authority? I think it may be time to speak to the union about all that."

Alexandra: "I've been wanting to move up from my job for a long time. I work in a financial investments company. My goal is to become a certified financial planner. I started as a temp three years ago, mostly as a filing assistant, but I've been taking courses at night in financial planning and I never miss a guest speaker at lunch or a chance to sit down with one of the investment counselors and pick their brains. I feel confident I can be a very good planner. I've just got to convince someone to let me into the training program."

Lucy: "How dare they? I put in for a transfer to go from the scheduling department to the marketing department six months ago, and now I see they've hired twelve new people, all from the outside. After I submitted that application I never heard another word. I don't think there's a chance in hell for someone like me to advance in this company. It's hopeless."

The answers to this exercise should be pretty obvious. I tried to make them that way because I was more interested in making clear the contrast between an employee mentality and a partner mentality than in tripping you up! So we'll score all of you an A on this latest quiz.

As you can see, the employee tends to be passive and willing to follow orders and just do what's expected (like Harriet). When an employee does go beyond minimal expectations, he does things like fill out applications and follow "proper" procedures, but then faults others or the entire system when no one notices (Lucy). The employee also refuses to take risks and even feels justified in not doing so. The rationale seems to be that as long as he is doing what he's been told to do, he ought to be taken care of (Thomas). The employee's attitude is one of entitlement.

A partner, instead, intuitively knows that no one's going to take care of him or her. The partner sees that to succeed and advance she has to get herself noticed by initiating ideas and going out and finding someone in authority who'll pay attention (Keith, Suzanne, Alexandra). No one's going to make it easy for the partner who realizes this. The true partner just has to believe in what he or she is doing and go out and risk rejection.

A partner's idea might be to contribute an improvement to a current system, like greeting visitors in the reception lobby (Suzanne), or it might be more personal, such as getting enrolled in her company's training program (Alexandra). A partner also appreciates the value of helping out by asking colleagues what they need (Keith), then getting involved in whatever challenges will give him the chance to grow. He enhances professional value in the marketplace by this behavior and affords decision makers an opportunity to see what he can do.

WHAT CAN YOU CONTRIBUTE?

How to Be the Perfect Partner

In business, everyone's always looking for a perfect match. Where can we find customers who really want our product or service? How closely does your resume match the job requirements spelled out in that Monster.com listing? How can two business partners complement each other, that is, make certain their individual skills and temperaments add up to a good team?

So you must also look for such a match when exploring new directions. What problems or needs have been waiting for someone to come along and help with them? Then when you find one, you'll next want to ask, "Could that 'someone' be me?"

In the Chinese written language, the symbol for *crisis* also signifies *opportunity*. That is the way you want to be thinking when you scurry about in search of your match. Specifically, ask yourself these questions:

"What problems at my place of work need to be solved?"
"What projects have been on hold, waiting for someone to help get them started?"
"What new ideas could dramatically improve profits and customer relations?"
"What new systems could be implemented that would speed up service and/or cut costs?"

These questions should give you the general idea. Any help you can offer your company or a department or manager that would improve the way things are currently done, or increase business, or solve a major problem, or fill a need, or get something started may be an "opportunity match" waiting to happen. A decision-maker gets busy at work and doesn't always have the time or energy to pay attention to everything that needs to be done. Her secret prayer is that someone will suddenly come along and offer competent assistance and a sackful of fresh ideas. That's where you come in.

And this goes double for the job seeker! Determine your value and go looking for not just a job slot but an opportunity to offer that value to a company that does not currently employ you. Make them discover your value to them… and as a result *hire* you!

Finding Your Opportunity Match

One day, Sharon Casey, an assistant to the VP of Operations at a biotech firm in South Carolina, finds herself sitting at lunch with the company's lab technicians. Before long, she's lunching with them two or three times a week and talking with them about the work they do. After about a month of this, Sharon realizes she's been really looking forward to these lunches and that she never tires of hearing about projects, adventures, and the mishaps of life in the lab.

She begins to wonder about transferring there. At first, she figures all she can hope for is administrative work, pretty much the same as she is doing now in Ops. But Jim and Kim are the lab's two administrative assistants, and they don't seem to be planning on leaving anytime soon.

One day at lunch, one of the technicians mentions a research project he's been wanting to get funded for a long time. He feels certain that his idea meets all the criteria required by the pertinent government agency, but he's been so swamped lately he hasn't been able to complete the paperwork.

Boing! Sharon has a brainstorm.

"Tim," she begins, taking him aside. "I think I might be able to help. What if I worked with you to complete the paperwork? I'm sure if you

WHAT CAN YOU CONTRIBUTE?

just showed me how to fill in the forms I could do most of it for you. We could get enough of your proposal in shape so you could finally submit it for funding."

Tim has been looking for the time to spend on this for some months now, not to mention someone who could help him make sense of the complicated government requirements. So Sharon's offer is a dream come true.

"I really appreciate this," he says. "Yes, of course, I'll accept your help. But, Sharon, may I ask why you would be doing this? It's only going to cost you more time and trouble on your end."

Sharon now has a clear response. "Tim, I've been lunching with you and your co-workers for over a month now, and I can't believe how fascinated I've become with what you all do. In fact, it's gotten me more interested in what the whole company does. Why, last week I read our annual report cover to cover, and I've even begun subscribing to a couple of industry trade magazines. I sometimes imagine myself working in the research department because it sounds like so much fun. I guess what I'm saying is this: If you ever hear of any position in the lab that I might qualify for, I'd love to be considered for it."

Tim thinks for a moment and then says, "You know, if this funding comes through for me, I'll need a research partner." Butterflies begin bustling around the walls of Sharon's stomach. "You might need to do some grunt work for me too," he continued, "but there'd be definitely lab work I'd need help with, which you could learn. So I would see you as a full-fledged *partner*."

Sharon had thus found her opportunity match. By hanging out with folks who interested her, and doing things that interested her, she had found herself reading up on lab issues and learning more about that kind of work. When the time came that she heard about a problem she could help with, she volunteered her services. She then made known her personal goals. By that point, her new partner, Tim, had become more than willing to help her out.

Is this really a one-in-a-million scenario? Is it unlikely you would ever run across a similar situation in your life? Was Sharon Casey merely lucky?

The answers to all three questions are a definitive NO, NO, NO! Scenarios similar to this happen every day, most of them, by the way, also starting out with the partner wannabee disbelieving that something like this could happen to *them*. Yet, after they launched their career advancement campaign and got it in gear, something just like this eventually happened.

However, by way of paying slight homage to your skepticism, let us add the following: Although this kind of scene *can* play itself out as easily as I've depicted, and although it will do so much more often than you might think, never, never, never *expect* it to.

You see, expectation tends to foster a passive frame of mind. We sometimes get a little too comfortable when we expect something to happen. We don't try as hard; we don't do as much. Don't believe me? Check out the dictionary definition of the word "expect." Among entries you'll find include "to wait," "await," and "to consider probable or certain."

When it comes to career advancement, however, you can't lay back and fall prey to expectation. You've got to put out an effort of 110%. No make that 1000 and 10%! There are so many potential forks in the road, ruts, falling boulders, discouraging words that you can't let your guard down for one ... pesky ... treacherous ... moment! Passivity has no place, nor does waiting or feeling overconfident or getting too comfortable.

So the key is *not* to expect *anything*, to instead expect *nothing*. That's right nothing. Do not expect, but rather prepare for the worst and go all-out for the best. That will always—always! —yield some kind of result. It may in fact not even be the result you sought (though it probably will) but at least you will have achieved *something*, and something is better than nothing. You will be achieving rather than passively laying back waiting and expecting.

So our CareerScape motto goes like this:

Expect Nothing
Achieve Much
Enjoy Everything

The last bit is the best, really. Why go through life in a quandary or depression? Why not enjoy the journey of getting from here to there? Why not forgo a life of disappointing expectation and instead spend it brimming with achievement? And if that is the way things will go, why not alleviate a little stress by enjoying the process? Yes, you will get there, so don't worry, be happy.

Let the steps Sharon Casey took serve as a shining example. Here's how she handled it:

1. *She observed.* What did Sharon notice that was not working well in Tim's department? What could be improved in *your* work environment? You don't have to have all the answers in hand at first. You just need to develop a knack for spotting problems.

2. *She located the bloke in charge of the problem.* Sharon had heard Tim grousing about a project he couldn't find time to get off the ground. His project sounded like it needed a certain skill (help with paperwork) that she could offer him. *That* was her cue.
3. *She decided what role she genuinely wanted to play.* If there is such a role for you too, make your wants public. If Sharon had heard of a similar need in the accounting or the marketing department, would she have volunteered to help there too? Probably not. Her excitement was aimed at the research lab because that was the place she wanted to end up. Tim's need for help that she could provide offered the opening she needed to get her there.

Sniffing Out Trouble

There once was a cardiothoracic surgeon in New York City who'd become renowned around his OR for sniffing out trouble. Many times he'd ask a resident physician or nurse about something that wasn't feeling right to him, and to go hunt down the problem. But when said resident or nurse failed to uncover the problem, Dr. Bob refused to accept that. "No, no… There's something wrong around here," he'd mutter, "and I'm going to find out what it is." Then he invariably proceeded to do so.

You should emulate this surgical bloodhound! You should determine that there's "something wrong" or at least there's a problem that needs to be dealt with … and *you* are precisely the guy or gal to sniff it out and fix it.

The good news about this career strategy is that, for a company in specific and the world in general, there will *always* be problems. There's always an abundance of needs to fill and there always will be. So you can feel quite confident that a true career match is in your future. You just have to look for it.

WHAT CAN YOU CONTRIBUTE?

On a sheet of poster paper, put together a mind map focusing on how your company is doing, or how a company you would like to work at is doing, so far as you can surmise. Include good things but don't forget to also include any problems, needs, or crises that come to mind. Write the company's name in the center and branch out with your wavy lines and tentacles as you did in previous mind maps. Just see what you come up with.

NOTE: If you are thinking of moving to another company, or if you are unemployed and targeting a number of companies, use only one of these target companies for this exercise. To use them all might make the mind map too complicated and confusing.

Read Thoroughly

Your next step is to read. Get ahold of your company's annual report, the company press kit, the company newsletter—any information that your targeted company publishes about itself. Read this material thoroughly and visit every single page of the company website. Take notes as you read, noting those areas of the organization that interest you. Ask yourself if you could imagine working on this or that project, or in such and such a department.

Next, get a little critical. Do you agree with everything you're reading? Do you disagree with anything the company is doing, or the way it's doing it? Can you spot any flaws in the company's thinking or strategy? Did you notice any missing pieces? Put the whole company under your personal microscope.

Next go back and add these latest thoughts and critical notions to your mind map.

More Stuff to Read

In addition to whatever printed materials you can get, Google around and see what you else can find. Look up books on Amazon and magazine articles on the web not only on your targeted company but on said company's industry too, and then on similar companies, and on the field or profession you've become interested in. If you're not sure how to find any of this, hop right over to the nearest library and ask a reference librarian for help with your career research. Before long that reference librarian will have become your newest BFF. So don't forget to send her a yummy fruitcake right around Christmas time.

Next go back and add to your mind map anything you find of great interest. Note relevant findings and quirky details. Make your mind map bloom and grow!

Career Conversations

Most books on career exploration use the term *informational interview* to indicate a technique for learning more about an intriguing job, career, company, or industry. But informational interviews typically denote one-on-one Q&A sessions, usually conducted in person at a formally appointed time and place (or perhaps by phone or email). The interviewer, either a potential career changer or a job seeker, asks the questions. The interviewee, usually a manager or other successful expert or decision-maker, patiently (and kindly) answers.

Informational interviews may take place in the interviewee's office or by phone for about 20-30 minutes (that's the recommended amount of time to request) though they frequently run longer once the interviewee starts feeling comfortable and even excited, and thus gets on a roll. When it's all over everyone shakes hands (literally or figuratively) and the interviewer thanks the interviewee, then leaves (or hangs up).

WHAT CAN YOU CONTRIBUTE?

Really conscientious, appreciative and *wise* interviewers follow up with a thank-you card in the mail or at least (next best thing) a follow-up email, within a day or two. Most of the time, after that, the two never see or hear from each other again, according to information interview custom.

Care for my opinion of this process? Two words: *hate it!* Not the process exactly, not the point of it and not the recommended appreciative thank-you but more so the form in which it's conducted. Here's what I mean:

The informational interview format tends to limit, not enhance, your chance to build valuable career relationships. IMHO, it's constricting, limiting, and boxy, setting up a dynamic between both parties that tends to stunt continued growth, as in: "OK, you got what you want; good luck to ya!" That might as well be what the interviewer hears when she leaves the interviewee's office, because that's usually the attitude. After all, the interviewing career explorer only asked for this *one-time* get-together.

The other problem with the informational interviews is that sometimes (though not always) too many people are out there doing them! Many professionals thus get bombarded with such requests and end up formulating canned rejections so that they won't find themselves giving away so much of their precious time. So voicing your request by specifically using the words "informational interview" raises a red flag and sets such a rejection response into high gear.

As an alternative to the informational interview, I suggest the "career conversation." Can you see a difference already, simply in the tone of this term vs. the other? Informational interviews—bad! Career conversations—good!

How might you compare these two techniques just by the sound of each term's words? What does the very name of each imply? Why do you suppose I would feel so strongly that a career conversation would have it all over the so much better-known informational interview?

In the list below, cast your vote for which technique—informational interview vs. career conversation—seems to better fit the characteristic cited. Keep in mind the sound per se of each technique's name as you deliberate your answers. Mark II or CC after each characteristic listed.

Conducted frequently on neutral ground
Two-way communication
Could be loose time frame
Generally by appointment only
Communication very formal
Generally on unfamiliar territory

If you marked CC for the first three and II for the bottom three, then you were thinking what I've been thinking. Career conversations offer more latitude (much more!) for getting to know someone since you could be conducting one off-the-cuff virtually anywhere—at a social gathering, at a professional event, in the supermarket, on the sidewalk outside the post office. Good communication is of course a two-way street—you yak, they yak, you yak again, they yak some more. There's a loose time frame, too—the fact of your yakking *together* means the yakking ends when it ends, i.e., when it's time to end. Everybody's doing what comes naturally.

Informational interviews, on the other hand, carry on just as the title implies, often stiff, formal, clinical, bounded by time. You meet on alien turf, which helps you get to know your interviewee's surroundings (a good thing this) but which also tends to set up an unequal dynamic for you. It's as if you're this poor, sad sack, career waif. You go out and meet people in *their* offices but they never come to yours.

It must be added however that going to your interviewer's office can also be a very advantageous thing to do, since you may end up meeting other people who work there, getting a tour, being treated like an honored guest. It can represent a first step into this environment, which may lead to more steps (and eventually the ultimate step: employment!). So going to your interviewer's workplace is not by any means all bad.

However, an informational interview's communication dynamic is often arranged within a very rigid format, which is a negative as well: You question the big expert and he deigns to answer you, for a short time at best (or at least that's the plan). "I can give you 15-20 minutes, OK?" you're told. Time is money!

An informational interview is thus so often set up on uneven terms that it's bound to foster a lower self-image on your part. That's the last thing you need when you're working to keep up both your spirits and optimism during frustrating or confusing career explorations.

Instead, what you want to feel is that you are the equal of other professionals. You want *not* to feel they're lords and ladyships while you're merely a lowly peasant. What's best is to encounter colleagues, teammates, fellow experts, hard-working working stiffs just like you: potential partners!

Would you call Sharon's exchange with Tim an II or a CC? It was obviously a CC all the way! In fact, since she'd been lunching with Tim and his colleagues for months, Sharon had been having rounds and rounds of career conversations with them for that whole time. What better way to gather the information you'd normally be seeking from informational interviews when at the same time you're building deep friendships with professional experts themselves?

By the time Tim's time problems came to light during their lunch conversations, for example, Sharon's own competence had become firmly established in Tim's eyes. Can you imagine how different the exchange might have been had Sharon experienced only a brief, stuffy, 20-minute informational interview exchange with Tim five or six months before? Can you imagine how much less would have happened?

IMAGINE THIS: Sharon is speaking to Tim over the phone:

Sharon: Maybe you don't remember me, but we met five months ago in your office.
Tim: Um, hmmm. I can't remember exactly, sorry. But what can I do for you?
Sharon: Well, I, uh, I heard you might be looking for a research assistant sometime soon and I wanted to apply for the job.
Tim: Oh, uh… what kind of experience do you have working in a lab?
Sharon: Well, none really. I'm, ah, an assistant over here in operations. But I'm very willing to learn and very interested!
Tim: Well, you know, the funding hasn't come through yet, and frankly I don't know when it will. But if you send your resume over to Human Resources, they'll hold it for me.
Sharon: Yes, well, I'll do that. I appreciate your talking to me. Thank you very much for your time. I'll send my resume out today.

WHAT CAN YOU CONTRIBUTE?

Does the phrase *snowball's chance in hell* come to mind here at all? Sharon will never hear from Tim or HR again… trust me!

So look for ways to get to know people, that is, to *really* get to know them. Combine your research techniques with less formalized relationship building so that people will remember you and understand what you can do for them and how you might fit in. This will lead to their becoming willing to take a chance on you. Rely however on the more distant, impersonalized, standard informational interview method and you'll rarely achieve this, faced instead with a challenge of continually trying to close up a relationship "gap."

NOTE REGARDING FORMAT: Although I emphasize here the in-person format of a career conversation (or information interview for that matter), you should not get hung up on that particular detail. Yes, it's the optimum situation, however if you find your career conversation "target" does not seem either willing or able to meet with you face-to-face (maybe they mention they are currently swamped with their own work, the most likely remark), then ask if you can do it either by phone or email. The latter is perfectly fine since you can email 4-5 questions (no more, please, don't overload this contact, especially if they have expressed they are squeezed for time) and will probably respond this way with sufficient information to help you along.

Always nudge them after a week or so if they have not yet gotten back to you, e.g., "Hi Mr. Pearson, Just wanted to be sure you actually received this email below which I sent to you last week. Thanks again for helping me out!" That will typically remind them to bring this task to the top of their to-do list, and (it must be added) *they will not be upset with you for so reminding them!*

And always thank them for sending back their answers to your questions, with this final line: "And if there is anyone you know who could also help me, I would appreciate the referral. I will put you on my e-list and social media so we can stay in touch and so I can let you know how my career search is going. Thanks again!"

SECOND NOTE REGARDING FORMAT: Making your initial contact via email is probably best, as it is less intrusive than calling out of the blue. But should you prefer or need to actually telephone, be ready for your new contact to say, "Well I'm very busy these days but I could talk to you NOW. What do you want to know?" Thus always be prepared with a few questions (only a few) so you can make the most of such a sudden opportunity. As well, ask if it would be OK if you could email him/her so that you can "send a follow-up question if I think of one and also keep you informed about my career progress." You want to grow and grow your e-list (and LinkedIn too) so that your career ally network will continuously expand and stay active. This includes AFTER you land your next position. More on this in Chapter 11.

Thanking everyone for their help at the end of a job search once you land something, and informing them which job and employer you have obtained, is both classy and unusual. Most people, believe it or not, don't bother! Suddenly most people can't find the time to thank those who have helped them along the way. Don't YOU become one of them!

6

POSITIONING YOURSELF FOR NEW SUCCESS

You've got to be careful. There are those who will help you and those who will not. Professionals in every corner of the workworld encounter the tendency of others to pigeonhole:

"You're an engineer, you say. What could you possibly know about advertising?"

"You're in advertising, you say. What could you possibly know about training and development?"

"You're in training and development, you say. What could you possibly know about financing?"

"You're in finance, you say. What could you possibly know about engineering?"

"You're a liberal arts major, you say. What could you possibly know about…anything?"

Your image as whatever you currently are thus has to be dealt with every day. As you begin to build those vital career relationships, you can't be too careful about ensuring that you're seen the very way you want to be seen. Stereotypical thinking runs deep. You must always aggressively clarify what you can do and what you're looking for. You must not take any prisoners ever again. Even your very best allies may *want* to help, but not know how. So it's your job to show them.

Leading Your Allies

When I say it's your job to show people what you can do, I mean you often have to literally lead them. Help others understand exactly what they can do for you… then drill it into them again and again.

"Do you understand what it is I really do?" This may be one early question to ask any potential ally. Should they say "yeah sure, of course," ask them to articulate it. Very likely, no matter what they say, they won't know how to paint your abilities and potential in as attractive or marketable a way as you could. They may get close but it never hurts to fine-tune. It's literally your *job* at this point in your career life to help them to do this.

Watch how Martin has done it:

THE EDUCATION OF AN ALLY

Martin has been working in the shipping department of a major manufacturing plant in Virginia. As he begins exploring other options inside the company, he finds himself drawn toward the inspection department. The idea of checking product samples *before* they're shipped intrigues him very much. He also is drawn to the camaraderie he's observed in that department. The potential increase in pay ain't too shabby either!

So Martin makes lunch plans with Merle, the department's chief inspector. Although Merle has no authority to hire him, Martin feels

POSITIONING YOURSELF FOR NEW SUCCESS

that talking with Merle may give him a clearer picture of qualifications needed to become a new inspector. Best of all, Martin gets Merle to accept his invitation to buy him lunch simply by being candid.

"I'm quite interested in learning more about your department," he tells him. "I'm finding myself more and more curious about possible career opportunities there. And since you've been there the longest, I thought it might make sense for me to ask you a few questions over lunch. Again... my treat."

Merle's first response is that he doesn't think there are any openings in the department at the present time. Besides, he doesn't handle the hiring himself.

"That's OK," Martin responds. "I'm not looking to apply right yet. I just want to learn more."

"Oh, well OK then," says Merle. "How about tomorrow at eleven-thirty in the cafeteria?"

The next day, as they sit down to lunch, Martin again summarizes for Merle why he wanted to meet with him. As is often the case when potential career allies are first approached for help, Merle had assumed that Martin was anxious to actually apply for a job here and now...and he also assumes that Martin would hope to do something in the department akin to his current shipping position, like a stock or inventory manager.

"You know, I'd like to help, I really would," Merle drawls, "but to be honest I don't think our department's stockman will be leaving anytime soon. He's been with us about twenty years, and he tells me he's now hanging on for the retirement benefits."

[*Time for Martin to educate Merle, again. Merle, like most potential allies, needs to have it explained what your intentions and inclinations are at this moment. Sometimes it takes three or four attempts before they get it. That's because Martin's request is not the usual straightforward one, as in: "Can you get me a job?" Instead Martin is appealing to Merle's experience so he can obtain from him opinions, news and guidance. So actually applying for a job will come down the road.*]

"Merle," he begins carefully, "what I'm actually interested in is leaving my work in shipping and doing something else. I've been investigating lots of options recently. The inspection department has come to interest me the most. Who knows? Maybe I'll become an inspector someday, like you!"

Merle stabs at a forkful of his salad and shovels it in. Chuckling nervously, he says, "With all due respect, Martin, I don't know if this would be the right job for you. You see, there's not as much lifting and moving around when you're an inspector like me. You've got to pay attention to tiny details, stay at your worktable and have great eyesight. You're always searching for defects in the material. It requires an awful lot of finger dexterity so you can pluck out a bad wire or circuit or other stuff as soon as you see it. So the question is whether you would have the right skills and personal attributes for this line of work."

[*Notice how Merle has pigeonholed Martin by the shipping work he does now, comparing it to his inspection duties. He doesn't mean to, he is just calling it as he sees it. In fact, he'd probably be the first to say that he himself wasn't especially qualified for inspection work when he first got the job. He too had to learn the ropes and work at it. But now that he's been there a while, it all seems perfectly natural to him so he forgets that he wasn't a BORN inspector. It's as if the skills and talents we utilize in our current jobs couldn't possibly be transferred to any other line of work.*]

POSITIONING YOURSELF FOR NEW SUCCESS

"Merle," he asks, "how much do you know about what I do?"

"Well," Merle replies confidently, "if I understand it right, you pick up boxes of varying sizes, toss them into a truck, maybe push a dolly-full of larger boxes into trucks, direct traffic out in the loading dock area, approve purchase and pick-up orders… like that. I'm sure you're darn good at it too."

"Thanks, Merle," Martin says. "I appreciate the compliment."

"Not at all," says Merle, smiling.

"But though you're correct at much of what you said, I also do some of the same things you do in the inspection room."

Even though well underway with his tuna sandwich now, Merle is listening hard. "You do?" he asks. "How so?"

"Well, think of it like this: Whenever I have to move a box, I have to pay close attention to the delivery slip attached as well as the requisition form I've been given. Do the two match up? Then sometimes we actually have to open the box and get into it, carefully survey all the contents and compare them with the specs in the paperwork.

"So in a certain sense, I'm paying attention to tiny details too, just like you in your inspection work. I've got to have a good pair of eyes for this too, I spot a lot of discrepancies I'll tell ya. I've saved the company a ton of money at times from potentially big mistakes."

Merle is impressed. "Hadn't known about that part of your job," he says, swigging his diet soda. "You know, I'd say from what you're telling me, with a little bit of training and some practice, you'd do real fine down on the inspection team! Can you come over now and let me show you around? I could introduce you to my boss too. Who knows? He's actually been thinking about adding a few trainees in the next month or two, now that I think of it."

See how you can't take anyone's supposed understanding of what you do for granted? In the same vein, you certainly can't take for granted the notion that other people will automatically envision your value to them. It's great when it happens on its own of course—when someone spots you or "discovers" you like they do movie stars—but my practical advice to you is this: never plan on it. Instead, carefully, methodically, patiently lead your allies through the quagmire of seeing you as the fully valuable, evolving professional you are. Your image in your current situation by no means represents all you can do, and your allies need to be patiently guided to the point of understanding this.

Leading HR

You won't necessarily have an easier time explaining yourself to a human resources department but you should plan to utilize them as best you can anyway. For example, they usually know of present and future openings in a company so they can be a storehouse of valuable information … if, that is, they share it with you!

To work with HR effectively you need to conduct yourself the same way you do when you're working with your career allies, perhaps even more so. HR folks after all are trained to think in terms of demonstrated skills within your work history, so an inquiry or proposal to be given a chance to take on some completely new challenge in their organization may fall on deaf and extremely perplexed ears. Merle's reactions in many ways echoed what you'll find from even the *least* seasoned HR pro. Worse than that, HR will first want to review your resume, a document that proclaims and arranges your professional credentials in a way you'd probably prefer *not* to display. A resume sends HR specialists settling on a snapchat of you from your past while you're imploring them to open up a new picture of you from your future.

It might be of value to you, then, to take a moment and reflect on how you might explain your "transferability" to HR, the toughest critic of them all. How can your particular past and current skill set be viewed as a plus in some new career area? How can you refocus your career value in a totally different direction? How can you make others see what you see?

Refer back to Martin's self-promotional explanations and responses to Merle if that would help as it showed his careful attention to details. Also, use a dream career direction (DCD) too if that helps as a kind of guide for the following exercise. If you're currently considering more than one DCD, choose just one at a time so as to keep this exercise simple. You can then do the exercise again and again with the other DCDs you are exploring. **NOTE:** To do this exercise meaningfully, you'll of course need to know at least a few of the skills and talents your DCDs entail.

On a sheet of 8x11 paper, first make a list of 4-7 of your current career skills. Then beside or below each one, explain why this skill would be a "plus" in your newly targeted DCD. If you have trouble figuring out a plus, replace with a different current career skill. Don't stop until you determine at least 4 pluses.

Visiting Other Departments

Back to Martin now. He'd made it a point to get to know someone in a department he was interested in, then followed up with a visit there. He saw Merle's operation up close and personal, which helped further identify that he indeed wanted to work there. Remember that sometimes things in life fail to live up to our prior images, work being certainly no exception. So it was crucial that Martin physically experience this potential new workplace in order to proceed to his next step, that of actually applying for a job there.

Of course, Martin had it easy, right? Since Merle had invited him over to visit the department, Martin didn't even have to raise the issue. But that's in fact a typical scenario when you do it right: Upon developing an enjoyable career relationship with someone, you will next experience that this new ally wants to help you in any way possible, surprising you with such invitations to visit the company or department, introducing you to just the right people, even confiding in you word of upcoming, still unannounced job openings. Merle ultimately offered all of these and more.

And it can get even better than that. Richard Bolles, author of *What Color Is Your Parachute?* used to include an experiment in career workshops in which he would send all his attendees out to do informational interviews with complete strangers. But not just any strangers, specifically strangers who were working in positions of authority at companies that a workshop attendee knew he/she definitely did *not* want to work for.

Choose companies that do things you know you don't care about, was his basic instruction. And don't call ahead for appointments, he would add, just drop in unexpectedly, then ask to speak to a manager or someone else in authority. Conduct your informational interview with them for only about 15-20 minutes, asking about the work they do and how they like it, what they don't like etc. Then thank them and leave.

Well, you can imagine the pessimism and shaking of heads in the room as attendees were given these instructions. Few of course believed they would ever get past the receptionist, much less attain a meeting or interview without a prior appointment. Even fewer imagined anything useful could come of this assignment. "Why would I want to talk at length to someone doing work I don't care about?" they wondered aloud.

Yet three hours later, all returned… chattering, excited, bushy-tailed, transformed. When Bolles asked the whole group "How did it go?" stories began to flow, many of them ranging from remarkable to miraculous.

"I got right in and spent an hour with a CEO," someone would say.

"I was treated to a tour of a company's entire facility," another would typically report.

"I met everyone who worked for this company," exclaimed others.

Invariably, *more than one* would announce: "I got offered a job!"

"Me too." "Me too." "And me." "Me too!"

Bolles has said as many as 20% of a workshop's attendees might have the same experience. A job, a job, a job… they got offered a real job!

So how could this have happened? Had attendees asked for these jobs? Had they feigned interest in working for the companies they were visiting? Had they announced that they were job hunting? Had they handed over resumes, somehow turned their informational interviews into job interviews?

Typically answers to these questions were no. Instead, each attendee had followed Bolles' instructions to the letter, so that the dynamics of natural human interaction could take over, which went like this:

By merely presenting themselves in a nonthreatening way, simply conducting themselves as curious and motivated individuals, by showing a sincere interest in the companies they were visiting, they had enabled their "hosts" to make judgments about their informational interviewers for themselves.

So if a job opening existed at that moment, or a need to be filled, or a problem that hadn't yet been solved, these company decision-makers may have been wishing, perhaps subconsciously, for "the right person" to walk through their doors and save the day. Even though these "right persons" visiting them today had not expressed any direct desire whatsoever to work for this company, the manager meeting with them perceived their potential. So you could almost hear the wheels turning and burning in their heads:

"Hmmm, I've a hunch about this lady. I don't know much about her but she seems to have a lot on the ball. Maybe she could handle this Allentown account for me. Maybe she could fix this problem. Hmmm… I wonder if she'd be interested in working here? I wonder if I could convince her to come aboard." Then, a decision to reach out. "I guess it wouldn't hurt to ask."

POSITIONING YOURSELF FOR NEW SUCCESS

In your own efforts, then, to explore opportunities that might be all around you, begin arranging meetings with people in their offices or making dates for what I call "opportunity luncheons" (or opportunity coffees or breakfasts) in the company's cafeteria or at a nearby café or a comfortable luncheon spot. Explain to those you approach that you're curious about the work they do because you're conducting "career education research" for yourself. For that reason, you'd like to sit down sometime and talk about their work, their departments, their co-workers—anything that would familiarize you with their career area, which has come to intrigue you.

Don't worry at first about *whom* you meet with. You could meet at first with a secretary or admin for example to get yourself warmed up. Visit a department of any kind and with whomever gets you in the door, past the gatekeepers. You're then primed to naturally connect, even briefly, with influencers, potential colleagues, decision-makers. Getting inside also enables you to see firsthand how other departments operate, which sets you up for your next step. Questions you now can answer include:

"Do I want to learn more?"

"Am I still intrigued with this career (or company)?"

"Have I seen or met anyone in this initial surveillance whom I'd like to talk to again?"

Don't be afraid to pitch your "career education" idea to anybody and everybody. Sometimes we get intimidated by folks in high positions, or by those who seem so involved in what they're doing that they'd never grant us even the time of day. But like those attendees in Richard Bolles' workshops... you'd be surprised! When you strip away facades, people are just that: people! You'll be amazed at how approachable such "unapproachables" can really be.

NOTE OF ADVICE: When suggesting an "opportunity lunch" (or coffee or breakfast), always offer to buy. You may get waved off on this, but make a lunge for the check anyway. "Oh, it's OK, I really want to," you insist. "I appreciate the helpful advice you've been giving me." A playful thing to add is: "When we get together again, we'll go to a really expensive place and then I'll let *you* pay." Ha-ha. Good one. Your new career ally will appreciate that. Remember, the goodwill you'll create by asking for this meeting and then showing how much you appreciate it will stretch a long, long way toward solidifying this new relationship. Make someone feel you've taken advantage however and all your potential for more help in the future will go right down the drain.

Stepping Out

Once you feel ready to branch out and really dig right in cultivating career allies, here's a can't-be-beat vehicle you must not ignore: professional associations. Think of the beauty of this set-up: you can garner all the career conversations you could ever want right in one room without so much as a prior phone call or email. All *you* have to do is show up!

As well, in most cases you won't even have to approach people or struggle for chit-chat or substantive conversation. The folks in this magical room with you will already be on top of all that, i.e., they will do the approaching, they will get a conversation with you rolling, they will transition from chit-chat to topics of more import, such as "What do you do?" "What are you looking for?" "How's business?" or "How's the job search going?" etc. **NOTE:** If you're a shy person, this is an especially great place for you!

POSITIONING YOURSELF FOR NEW SUCCESS

So the only question is which professional association (or trade group) makes the most sense for *you*? Which represents your latest DCD? Which will bring you into contact with the perfect people with whom to conduct career conversations or perhaps even hear of a lead or two for an actual job?

Thinking of going into sales? There's undoubtedly a chapter of the Sales and Marketing Executives of America near you.

Contemplating academia? How about checking in on the local branch of the National Teachers Association?

Got your heart set on a DCD in banking? Attend the monthly meeting of the American Bankers Association in your area.

See, there's a trade group for every endeavor. Trust me, you could fritter away your valuable career time in many, many ways but participating in a professional association event, even if you just came and sat and quietly watched, isn't one of them. Here's what typically happens:

For an investment of maybe $20-30, you can stroll into a swanky hotel function room with your very own nametag on your lapel or around your neck, then immediately find yourself engaged in a friendly chat over by the hors d'oeuvres table. You'll soon be sitting at a big round table with 9 or 10 other professionals soaking up all kinds of informative tidbits and gossip about companies, trends, upheavals, exciting developments and major players in the industry or professional of your choice. And filling up your fat face with food and drink the whole time!

Effortlessly, you'll take part in many, many career conversations, you'll trade biz cards and contact info, you'll make new friends (read: career allies) plus you'll usually also be privy to a career-oriented educational program of some kind, likely with an expert in the field who has come to speak to you and your new allies on a topic that you all will find fascinating. After this great presentation, feel free to engage the speaker in a little chit-chat ("I really loved your presentation!" is an excellent way to begin) and trade contact info with him/her as well. Now you have a career ally who is prominent in your targeted new field. What more could you ask for?

Once you get the hang of this, you'll next want to move up the ladder and check out conferences and trade shows. Special events of this type go on all year, often sponsored by a professional organization's local chapter, maybe the very one that you just attended. But a conference deepens your involvement, chock-full as it is with even more active major players, useful and substantive presentations and panels, lots of jocular networking and camaraderie… in other words, heartfelt, invaluable career relationship-building.

BONUS #1: Actually join one of these organizations and you'll begin receiving mailings and eblasts that will alert you to more such events. This gives you the chance to enjoy the benefits of a professional association again and again and again.

BONUS #2: If you *really* want to rack up some serious mileage from your professional organization membership fee, also get involved behind the scenes. By volunteering for committee work or to edit the newsletter or to work the registration table, you'll build up your career allies list really fast. Plus, those inevitable resulting career conversations will dramatically increase your knowledge of and your intimacy with your chosen new field.

Making Your Boss Your Mentor

For those of you who currently work at a company you'd like to stay with, this section is for you. If instead you are jobless or aching to escape your current employer, you might just skip on down the road to the next chapter. ALTHOUGH ... these ideas might help you too, especially if there is someone in your life who might fit the bill as a potential mentor. So maybe you too should at least skim this section and see if there's any way you could apply its advice and principles.

For many folks, the concept of converting their current boss into their mentor seems as likely as a luxury vacation to Mars. Then again, if one keeps an open mind, one realizes that the technology to actually deliver humans to Mars is already here (yes, it's true, not funded or authorized of course but technologically speaking absolutely something we can do). Thus who knows what might happen if you set your mind to it?

It might even be that your boss has already given you signals that she's more than willing to mentor you, just that you haven't picked up on them. Or it could be that, given the right coaching (by you), he could get that way. Whatever the case, too many times we *assume* that our bosses have no interest in helping us along. Frequently nothing could be farther from the truth.

Some experts point out that without a boss's support, professionals must proceed quietly "and that's tough," explains HR expert Paul Falcone because "other managers probably won't even want to talk to you if they know your boss doesn't approve. But you probably *can* make your boss your mentor, which is the best scenario."

So how does one elicit such mentorship from one's boss? Let's take a little quiz:

1. Do you currently enjoy open, free communication with your boss? Can you talk to him, offer ideas, tell him when you're feeling overworked, confused? Does he give you time off when you need it?
2. Does your boss ever confide her feelings in you or ask you for favors? Does she offer to do favors for you? Does she ask you frequently how you are doing?
3. Does your boss offer to send you to training programs and outside seminars and conferences? Does he see you as a resource to be developed? Does he ever bring in outside consultants to train his staff (including you) and to help everyone grow professionally?
4. Is she patient with your mistakes? Does she recognize that learning takes time? Does she pitch in and help you whenever "crunch" time rolls around?

After reviewing these questions, what's your general reaction? Your boss doesn't have to do or feel *all* of these things. What we're talking about here is his or her potential. Consider:

Have you ever actually asked your boss to mentor you? Have you asked if he'll pay for a professional training you might be interested in? Have you asked if you could attend trainings that are not strictly related to what you do now, such as an accounting seminar, an engineering conference, a sales training program—something you're exploring and would like to learn more about?

Remember, in today's "post-job" society you've got to do all the initiating yourself. More people are willing to help you than you know, but you've got to pick up the ball and explain to them how to do so. *They* are not always going to know how, or whether, to proceed. Your boss is no exception.

If you're unsure about your boss-as-mentor, first test the waters. You may recall that Falcone advises that you start by seeking reimbursement and/or time off for a training program or workshop, especially one that is not in your current sphere of expertise. Find something that interests you, then propose the idea to your boss. If he says yes, you'll know you're on to something.

Your next step might then be to strike up a little career conversation about your interest in professional advancement in general— that is, what are her feelings about how people should try to get ahead in these difficult times? See what she says. If all this feels positive, take one step closer: Ask her about helping you out, explaining your goals. She may very well say yes.

And if your boss rebuffs the idea and gives the impression that professional advancement is instead only his or her purview and not yours? Well, then, yes you've got a problem. But not an insurmountable one, mind you, just a problem in search of an alternative solution.

What to Do When Your Boss *Won't* Mentor You

When your boss won't be your mentor, you have two clear choices:

(1) Find someone else
(2) Find a group of "someone elses"

For example: Is there a formal mentoring system in your company? If not, could you start one? You do have to be a little cautious here because you don't want a nonsupportive boss catching you spending too much of your time thinking about moving on, and not enough time working for him. But if you keep up with the day's workload in a cheery and energetic fashion, there shouldn't be any flack. Within a formal mentoring program, such an official structure should move things along nicely. Who could blame you for that, you, a mere participant?

On the other hand, if there's no formal structure and if you cannot start one, you'd best instead go about enlisting the aid of a mentor on the q.t. Not that you need to keep the whole thing top secret…just don't *broadcast* it. Do what you have to do, attend to your official responsibilities, pay meticulous attention to your current boss, but also, whenever and wherever possible, put in some time on your personal career needs as well.

Find Someone Else

Finding someone else will typically revolve around our number one career advancement technique, the career conversation.

So how can you use career conversations to find the proper mentor? That of course is a piece of cake: Just ask around.

Begin by asking people you know for mentor nominations "in confidence" of course. The very process of asking folks for help will enroll them in your career advancement campaign, by the way, involving many friends in such a way that *they'll* become impromptu mentors for you too, without your even asking. Imagine that, an "instant mentor" system— brilliant!

POSITIONING YOURSELF FOR NEW SUCCESS

Put together a list of criteria when you begin your solicitations. You'll want to find a mentor who's really right for you, after all, so what kind of person is that exactly? What profession, skill level, years of experience, personality type etc. do you want to find? There are some objective standards I could recommend but in the end it's you who's got to tailor your search for the match that's perfect for *you*. Much of it, of course, will be based on your gut reaction: "Do I like this person?" "Do I feel confident about her commitment to me?" "Do I respect his ideas?" But a list of criteria may help you reach a point where you can evaluate a lineup of finalists.

Alongside your personal mentor criteria, here are some other criteria ideas to keep in mind:

1. Pick someone who's *positive*. You want a mentor who will keep your spirits up during the downs as well as the ups.
2. Pick someone who's been *through the mill*. Success usually delivers less personal growth than failure. Find a mentor who understands that failure is a valuable ingredient in the mix and so can counsel you whenever it rears its all-too-familiar plug-ugly head.
3. Pick someone who understands that *credentials aren't everything*. Your mentor should be aware that change is here to stay and that upgrading our career value via continuous education will likely breed more success in the long run than leaning on past (read: outmoded) educational triumphs and learning. All knowledge is in flux.
4. Pick someone who *knows a lot of people*. One can't have too many career conversations or career allies or career friends you know! Much of your career success will rest upon the shoulders of others who get to know you. Find a mentor who fully understands this.

On the following lines, set down *your* criteria for a mentor who would be right for you. Jot down ideas that come to mind. What can you add to our list of "objective" criteria?

_____

_____

_____

_____

Appoint a Board of Mentors

Remember how earlier I suggested finding "two or more somebody elses" to serve as your mentors? Well, here's what I meant: Companies set up boards of directors to advise them on their business strategies, yes? Why not set up a board of directors for yourself whose members exhibit the same criteria you have in mind for your ideal mentor? We might call this vehicle your "board of mentors."

Certainly, two (or more) heads can be better than one. And more individuals invested in genuinely assisting you in your career advancement campaign are likely to result in a multiplicity of eyes and ears out there in the streets and in the suites looking out for you.

So scout around, if you're inclined, for more than one mentor. Maybe you'll set up a monthly meeting in which everyone gets two or three big, fat, juicy slabs of deep-dish pizza, courtesy of the chairperson of the board (you of course) and maybe a chance for each member to do some career advancement interaction of their own (with fellow other board members of course). You'll be surprised how much fun a technique like this one can bring to an otherwise overly solemn and stress-laden process.

Making Your Presence Known

When people get to know us and like us, they will do their best to help us, no matter what our backgrounds and personal stories. That doesn't mean they will sponsor us for a job we're not qualified for, or help us win a job that they doubt we can do well, but it does mean that they will probably sponsor us for a job we do seem to qualify for.

Thus a next order of business when seeking to extricate yourself from the career you are currently stuck in, or from your lowly status as a "recent college grad," is to get yourself as qualified as possible in the DCD of your choice... which you'll do by (a) returning to school, or (b) enrolling in a relevant training program, or (c) learning to explain how your current skill set is transferable, or (d) becoming an apprentice or assistant to an established expert.

As usual, you'll need to continue to build your career relationships. You can achieve this in ways I've been describing, but you can supplement this effort through any number of techniques that serve to make you much more visible in your DCD.

How can you do this? Easy! Just activate one or more of the following techniques:

- *Public speaking.* Almost everybody hates to do it, and even some celebrities (Carly Simon and Barbra Streisand, to mention two megastars) hate to get up in front of others, so much in fact that they've both been known to keep off of stages and platforms for literally years.

Thus those of us who push ourselves up there do stand out. An immediate credibility comes with getting up and standing tall and proud in front of others, even when we're visibly nervous or inexperienced. Because even then, many in the audience will at least say, "She's got guts to get up there." And that's how you want people to feel about you—that you're willing to do what it takes, no matter what.

So where can you "public speak," especially if you're just getting started? First, you can practice just by raising your hand at meetings and sharing your thoughts whenever you get the chance. That alone will help get you more comfortable with public speaking.

Secondly, you can volunteer to introduce other speakers at meetings, luncheons, weddings etc. and/or moderate or take part in panel discussions. This way you'll get practice getting up in front of a raging riptide of strange, unforgiving faces (or so you'll unfairly believe) without having to stay up there all that long. Just thirty seconds here and there, just that short a time frame, can help build your confidence *dramatically*.

Now, to push yourself farther and to really, really get into the swing of public speaking, join a Toastmasters Club at your local library. Or volunteer to speak at meetings and conferences sponsored by your relevant professional organization, church group, civic association etc. There are plenty of opportunities around. Stand up, speak up, and you'll be seen and heard by everyone.

- *Task forces and committees.* Is there a quality-control committee, a marketing-ideas committee, a customer-relations committee... anything that you as an employee can get involved in with others in your current company or professional association? If there is, then get on it! You'll substantially raise your visibility by interacting with others over substantive issues and by helping to make hard decisions and recommendations. Just one or two tours of duty here and there and you might even one day be elected the committee chair which is often there for the asking since most committee members would rather not take on the extra time nor the extra responsibility that accompanies such a commitment. So YOU grab it, which will *really* raise your visibility and credibility levels!

Remember too that this same technique works great when you're looking to gain visibility outside your company, or if you're unemployed or looking for a new employer. Join committees within your relevant trade or professional association to catapult you to career stardom. Consider also vying for a position on a board of directors that governs a private company or a nonprofit agency. Any of these ideas can seriously open doors to opportunities you would otherwise not have heard of.

- *Company newsletter.* Say, remember when you were editor of your high school yearbook? Or a reporter for your college newspaper? Guess what: you can do any or all of that all over again! And doing so will move your career ahead 20 paces.

The company newsletter (or your professional association's newsletter or e-letter) frequently gets overlooked as an effective vehicle for visibility. But think about it: You can write for it, edit it, take photos for it, get written about in it, get your photo taken for it, get an announcement about you printed in it, and on and on. Just take the view that you *love* publicity any way you can get it!

Make sure, of course, that any publicity you do get advances your professional goals and stature. For example, if you want to transition to management, write an article about new management techniques, or do a book review of a new management best-seller, or get yourself interviewed about management techniques used by you in your own work.

What to be beware of? That's easy: anything that reinforces your image as a specialist in the area you want to get out of, or pigeonholes you as a "recent college grad" or a "currently unemployed" professional.

Therefore, no articles or interviews about what you do *now*. Your purpose is to drag yourself forward. Don't affix lead weights to your ankles as you try to do so.

Whom Can I Approach?

In a notebook you've purchased just for this purpose (hint, hint), or an Excel grid or Google Drive grid etc., start listing everyone you can think of who might qualify as a career ally. List name, address, email, phone number, and various relevant professional and personal details.

Next, start categorizing according to priority. Who's an *A* whom you want to approach first, who's a *B*, who's a *C*? Some you might want to send a letter to first; others you'll just pick up the phone and call. Leave space to mark down what happens as you begin making contact. Who accepted your calls? Who returned your calls? Who agreed to meet with you? Who's been great? Who's been a dud? Keep accurate and complete records so that you learn who is best to contact for this question or that one, e.g., questions about particular departments, companies, hiring managers, professional groups. That's how the typical successful, high-achievement professional would go about this.

And you're of course rapidly becoming one of those.

Legion of Career Heroes
ELENA PETRICONE: Displaying her Value

As my unpaid summer intern, Elena Petricone, now my trusted editor (for the past four years) and professional sidekick, showed me how valuable she could be from day one.

During the initial meeting of my intern staff that first summer, Elena did something none of my other chosen interns bothered to do, not just then but for that matter any previous intern summer: she took notes! This made her stand out for me as the one who most cared about getting things done and getting them done right.

So right from the start, I involved her in major situations, including a trip to a client site a few days later. I had room for only one intern to come and I chose her.

As time went on, she continued to display her value, in one instance for example suggesting it might be a good idea to take my webinar PPT slides and post them on the company website as "slidecasts" for visitors to see, as well as on other appropriate websites so as to expand the reach of our Internet presence.

"Ah, OK, I'm open to this," I responded when she presented the idea, "but just one question: What's a 'slidecast'?" She explained it was simply another term for my webinar's audio-visual presentation. "Hey, I knew that, I was just testing you," I joked. Yeah, right… as if.

But my second question was more crucial: "Do you know how to post these slidecasts on my website and on the other sites?" After all, I had sought interns who were primarily literary-oriented not techies.

"I don't but I can find out," came Elena's response. "I'll research it, I'm sure it won't be hard." Not hard for *you* anyway, I thought. Just don't ask *me* for any help. I hadn't a clue.

But given that I wasn't paying her anything, I had nothing to lose. "Go to it!" I commanded.

Before long, she had done her research, put in an hour or so on our company desktop, worked out a few glitches, then … voila! "They're posted now," she announced, "want to take a look?" Astonishingly, she had actually figured it out!

Throughout that summer, she added more and more value to my firm and its processes such that, by the end of the summer, I felt it only made sense for me to offer her a job. She's been with me ever since.

7

CAREER TREASURE CHEST

Rachel is beginning to get depressed. She's been a project manager at a small software company for about twelve years but she is desperately overdue for a change. Everywhere she looks, however, every new situation she locates, every potential employer to whom she applies sends back, in one form or another, the same message: "We'll keep your resume on file. Sorry, no openings at the moment."

In one way most every rejection relieves her. She doesn't want to continue as a project manager, applying for such positions only because she doesn't know what else to do. "What else am I qualified for?" she keeps asking herself.

But her depression really sets in when the volume of rejections reaches past 100. "Nobody wants you," they scream at her. "Stay where you are!"

Unfortunately, this very unpretty picture plays itself out each and every day in the lives of hundreds of thousands of otherwise very competent, very astute professionals. Its assumptions lie stuck-deep in outmoded ideas about how one looks for work combined with a low ebb of self-confidence, about one's chances for success in an entirely new field.

Sadly, most of us accept such stuck-deep assumptions as the "only way" or the only obvious or logical strategy.

We then justify our wrong-headed thinking by bursting out, once we can't take it any longer: "I don't know any other way to do this." Which I personally find rather interesting because, having counseled hundreds and hundreds of career professionals who have burst forth with this very frustration, I've heard it from veterans of all kinds who ought to know better, including, incredibly, formerly top sales pros, genius marketing gurus and even research experts. Come to think of it, I've heard it from so-called expert job hunting career counselors too!

All of these pros have matter-of-factly incorporated many of the exact same principles of carrying out a creative and successful career advancement plan in their current or past professional lives. But even they can fall prey to traditional, if ineffective, avenues of job search once they find themselves out there on their own. I'm talking about writing out a resume, checking online job postings, emailing legions of resumes… then doing not much else.

Assumptions that Need to be Challenged

1. I may apply only for work I've done before.
2. I must base most of my advancement plan on job postings.
3. The smartest thing is to dutifully send out my resume, then passively await a response.
4. Job hunting, by definition, is a lonely endeavor.
5. Lots and lots of rejection letters mean of course that nobody wants me.

Given these standard assumptions of how to go about the process, it's no wonder Rachel's spirits began to sink.

CAREER TREASURE CHEST

Upending Rachel's Assumptions

I don't really know where or when we all picked up the signals that got us into this wrong-headed assumption mess, but I do know this: If you're going to be effective in advancing your career, outmoded job search thinking has got to go, go, go! Rachel's no different from so many, many others, she just fell smack dab into the same trap that keeps most career explorers from scrambling back up onto solid ground and staying the course toward their dreams. I could sum up the problem with two insidious little words: *isolation* and *passivity*.

Rachel let herself buy the notion of her limited value to the marketplace. But we've seen how it's possible to extend your value in the marketplace and transform it into something new, something exciting, something refreshing, something conducive to growth. In the same way, we need to rethink tools, resources, job search techniques, and other "treasures" in our career treasure chests so they'll be more effective in advancing our dreams.

One way that might assist us in this world would be to outright challenge all of Rachel's assumptions.

Rachel's Assumption 1: I can apply only for work I've done before.

Flip Side: I will seek and embrace the work I really want.

As you gather together your board of mentors, meet with your career allies, and visit co-workers in other departments, you'll want to be sure you communicate what you most want them to hear. That means drawing conclusions from the research and career conversations you've been conducting thus far. So sit yourself down now (oh, some of you are already sitting, aren't you?) and contemplate the following "career questions." Provide any answers you've come up with on the blank lines beneath each question:

DISCOVER **YOUR DREAM** CAREER

1. *Of all the career options you've been exploring, which ones most motivate and excite you? List at least one but no more than three.*

_____

_____

_____

2. *What kinds of people would you most like to work with? Describe in detail the work atmosphere you'd most like to find.*

_____

_____

_____

3. *Where would you like your new situation to be located? How far from your home, in what direction? How much travel would you like to be doing?*

_____

_____

_____

4. *What kind of compensation are you looking for? Include your income goals as well as benefits, vacation time, investment options, health plan.*

_____

_____

_____

5. Where would you like to be in the future? Describe how you see your next position fitting into your career plans five years from now.

_____

_____

_____

Career Visioning

Now take these answers and craft your "career vision." On a sheet of poster paper, illustrate with colored markers or crayons exactly the kind of career move you want to make. Be sure to include *all* details listed above.

Now that you've finished your drawing, complete this phrase using the space provided below:

My career vision consists of…

_____

_____

_____

_____

_____

Congratulations! You are well on your way now to clarifying what you want!

Of course you will probably need to continue career conversations to flesh out many of these details or to refine them and to weigh how realistic this dream career idea of yours is. But no matter, as long as you keep thinking and wondering and writing down new ideas and then researching details, your career vision will become more and more real and attainable.

What if you listed more than one career option? Say you like two or three equally and you're beside yourself trying to figure out which one to really go after. Well, how's this next thought for a wild idea? Choose them all!

Many professionals today have caught on to a trick that businesses have been wise to for years. They call it diversification. In its simplest terms, this means that you commit yourself to a professional life that integrates two or more career areas at once so that you "diversify" it. In addition to allowing you to enjoy your overall worklife more, this approach offers a level of security that relying on only one source of income simply cannot beat.

Graduates of my programs who have gone this route include: a former executive admin who now offers a life coaching service during the day and serves up massage on nights and weekends; an ex-school administrator who now teaches Spanish at a community college while also running a dance studio; a former real estate appraiser who coaches high school athletic teams five afternoons a week while working part-time in a college admissions office during the mornings.

If, however, this "career mosaic" approach doesn't ring true for you, just keep exploring, researching, career conversing. At some point, you'll find yourself spending most of your energy on one or the other of your career directions. That may spell out your answer.

Rachel's Assumption 2: **Base your career advancement campaign on job postings.**

Flip Side: Use such postings as clues.

You've heard it before, I'm sure: Job postings represent only the tiniest percentage of the job market. Think about it: You know little about the job, little or nothing about the employer, nothing at all about who will interview you, little or nothing about compensation or the working conditions or the job's future.

Next, you're supposed to follow orders in the job posting to a T: Email your resume (no phone calls please) including your "salary requirements" as well as references from, well, just about everybody you've ever met. Say what? Shouldn't you crate your mother and favorite pooch or feline off to them too?

If you're looking for work *outside* your company, carry on exactly as I've advised you so far regarding methods for seeking a change *inside* your company—that is, build relationships and create visibility by conducting career conversations. High-energy, people-oriented day-to-day activities should absorb at least 80 percent of your efforts.

What do you do with the other 20 percent? Answer postings if you like but also use them as clues. Understand that job postings are somewhat like icebergs: You can easily see the very tip, but there's always a lot more where that came from beneath the surface too.

Let's say you're interested in working in customer service. You spot a couple of postings for customer service, so what you do next is make a note of the type of company that's doing the advertising.

Then after you've emailed your resume to these first two postings, you jump back on Google and check for similar companies under the theory that they might also be in the market for a good customer service rep.

Just don't call human resources! Instead call the customer service department directly. Strike up a friendly career conversation with one of the reps and then let her direct you to her manager. If there's a job available and if you're prepared to present yourself for it, you might be able to go for it then and there.

If instead you're still researching customer service work, however, ask to come in for a career conversation or an opportunity lunch. The key thing here, as I've been saying, is to build relationships.

Postings and other job ads, then, offer clues that the kind of work you're hunting down is definitely out there. Gather whatever data such ads *offer*, then file them in your memory bank. If you follow clues to companies that aren't even posting, you might end up meeting decision-makers who've been waiting and waiting, without knowing it, to meet you.

Rachel's Assumption 3: **Email your resumes and wait passively for a reply.**

Flip Side: Never even *use* a resume.

This one's a typo, right? Gotta to be a mistake. Maybe I'm just joking.

Actually, in fact… I mean it! If possible, *never* use a resume. You'll likely have way more success without one.

How can I say this? Have I gone wacky in the head? You've just *got* to have a resume, right? Everybody's got to have one.

Wellllll ….no. Yes, you ought to *have* a resume, I'm just telling you never to *use* it!

You see, it's like this. Many of the most successful dream career explorers have successfully switched careers in just this very way, i.e., without using a resume. In fact, many of the most successful people you've ever met, or heard about, gave up using resumes long ago. That's because the way they handle their career activities is through building career relationships, conducting ongoing career conversations, and participating in professional organizations. Such tactics make your standard garden variety resume totally unnecessary.

The deal is this: resumes generally get requested by people who still aren't sold on you. Instead of helping you get closer, your resume does the opposite, acting as a buffer or excuse for contacts who want to get off the hook (or off the phone). "Well, send me your resume and we'll talk again later." Blah, blah, blah. Yeah, right!

After sending said resume, you'll usually become a dead issue to such people—conversation over, resume filed, on to the next candidate (or project) for them. No further contact with you planned or anticipated. So if your resume does get a lengthy look-see, you'll probably be judged as not qualified for the position you're applying for.

And it's no secret why: Your resume trumpets, in great detail, the "you" who has spent many years in service to something else. Unless you've put your resume together very cleverly and creatively, it simply won't promote your potential, your enthusiasm, your ability to learn new things, or your burning motivation to grow. Rather than cast you in the accurate light of who you are today and who you can become tomorrow, it instead, sadly, works *against* you, depicting only one very limited side of you—your experience in the past toiling away in a different profession or in high school or college or in a low-level, go-nowhere position of the sort that suggests you are dead-wrong for this very different job.

Still and all—sigh!—there will be times when you really ought to have one. Even if you do everything I say in this book, such as building a vast empire of career relationships, here and there you may be asked for a resume in good faith.

Example: "I'd really like to get you into my department, Claire, but the company does require that I file your resume. So just let me have your resume as a formality and we'll be in business." Then: "Oh, and by the way: Welcome to my staff!"

At this point, you'll want to hand over a resume that speaks exactly to the reasons you're being hired, those characteristics you've sold your new boss on—your talents, relevant skills, enthusiasm, potential. You want your new employers to say, "Yessiree, here we have it: We hired the right gal!"

Resumes for Every Occasion

Another reason to have a resume, though—and in some ways perhaps your best reason—might be as an exercise to clarify further your new value in the marketplace. You can't ask yourself too often what you want, and likewise you can never get too clear about what you might offer a new employer. Revising your resume can substantially upgrade your understanding of your "work self."

Now what kind of a resume would be right for you? How can you display yourself as something other than what you've been for the past, oh, four years, ten years, twenty years? Well, since most of us have been schooled in resume-writing to put down everything we've done in our work lives starting from our present job and then listing all the others backward chronologically, then we're bound to be confused. Especially if we've grown up thinking that's the only way.

But another style of resume-writing exists, one that focuses on talents, abilities and achievements, and one that will work much better for a career explorer looking to make a move in a brand new dream career direction (DCD). Many career advisers call this a functional-style resume, but personally I find that term clinical and drab.

Example: "Tell me, chum, just what 'functions' do you perform on your present job?"

Heck, are we talking about machinery here or human beings?

So let's label this format a "success-style" resume and leave it at that. That will keep us thinking positively.

Success-Style Resume Close-Up

To get started, go back now through the exercises in previous chapters and take a fresh look at your talents, skills and achievements. How many of these are relevant to the exciting DCD you've come up with so far? If you've conducted plenty of career conversations and done lots of reading and googling, you'll have come up with a few answers.

Focus on only one career direction per resume. If you're thinking about going for two or more, you've got to fashion a resume to serve each. You should even plan to tailor your resume to particular jobs, companies, departments etc. Your career conversations will help you do this, by enabling you to understand particular priorities and values inherent in each situation. You then incorporate such information by mixing in what about *you* seems relevant to these, emphasizing your most significant attributes as they pertain to these priorities and values by placing them higher on the page. You should also drop irrelevant information about yourself entirely out of your resume so that doesn't get in the way or confuse.

Take a gander at this sample I've drawn up just for you...

Elizabeth Doolittle
5 Hartford Street
Hereford, New Hampshire 02119
603-555-1111, edoolittle@myfairlady.com

Achievements
- Coordinated over 100 focus groups consisting of up to 500 clients each (Alfred Beverage Company)
- Processed more than 10,000 customer survey projects, including tabulation of 3,500 customer service questionnaires (Alfred Beverage Company, Pickering Institute)
- Participated actively in Customer Response Committee (Rex Corporation)
- Administered and supervised correspondence of approximately 5,000 letters with major clientele (all employees)

Skills
- Excellent client liaison skills
- Knowledge of marketing-oriented customer relations
- Excellent administrative skills and software expertise

Professional History
- Client Service Coordinator—Alfred Beverage Company, Salem, New Hampshire
- Client Service Assistant—Pickering Institute, Manchester, New Hampshire
- Customer Traffic Manager—Rex Corporation, Londonderry, New Hampshire

Education
- Customer Service Skills Certificate—American Management Association Seminar
- Direct Marketing Skills Course—Hookset (NH) Junior College

- Communication Skills for Women—Manchester (NH) Adult Education Center
- Business Administration Associate Degree—Katherine Gibbs School, Boston—was graduated with honors

Personal Interests
- Treasurer, local chapter, Customer Service Association of America
- Greeter, Community Church of Hereford (NH)
- Author of *Guidelines for Good Member Relations*, a handbook for the Hereford, New Hampshire YWCA

What kind of work do you suppose Elizabeth (let's call her what her professor friends call her, Liza) is seeking? What work do you suppose she's best qualified for? Would you be likely to surmise from this resume that Liza has spent her entire career as a mere receptionist?

Yet there's nothing false about the way Liza has structured this description of her professional history and abilities, she's merely made it relevant to the work she's seeking. Her objective is to help potential employers see clearly how she can fit in.

The old school (Rachel's school) heaps all the onus for figuring out how you might fit in on someone else—a potential boss, manager, employer, human resources representative. Yet those folks can know only what you tell them about you. They can't for example know what new things you're capable of unless *you* make a case for it. Thus rather than waiting for a formal job interview to make such a case (as Rachel would do), you can get right down to the business of selling yourself in this resume.

Which only makes sense, of course, right? Because if you don't sell yourself from the get-go, how are you going to land that formal job interview in the first place?

Putting Your Success-Style Resume Together

To compose your own success-style resume, first loosen yourself up: wriggle your fingers and toes, roll your neck around a few times, shrug your shoulders up and down. People often get very tense about putting together their resume but the good news for you is: *You* don't have to! This document will instead truly liberate you, an expression of your dreams and of your Very Best Self. Really.

1. *List all talents, skills, and achievements you find to be relevant to your dream career direction.* Make this list as long as you like—you can cut it down later.

2. *List every single place you've ever worked in your professional life.* Put down a title for yourself first, then the name of your employer (or department) underneath. If possible, make sure the job title sounds as if it's connected to the kind of work you want to do next. Try to think of something that describes your work in this position accurately but slants it in your DCD. Don't just plunk down the title as your employer had identified it if you can help it... unless it indeed would sound good to your DCD associates.

You may need your present boss or a past one to back you up on your descriptive title. If he, she, or they won't do that, you'll have to make a judgment call. As long as you can make a case for the descriptive title you've put down, it'll probably be worth getting challenged about it if it comes to that. Obviously you don't want to just make stuff up... but you've got to find a way to sound like you've been steadily preparing for this DCD that you've set your sights upon.

Want an example? Look back at Liza's resume. In seeking a dream career direction in customer service, she labeled herself a client liaison in her two previous jobs and a customer liaison in her first job. In fact, these positions had been listed officially as administrative assistant, receptionist and lobby greeter, in that order. But those are no more descriptive of what she really did at each job than her more creative DCD-oriented titles. In fact, they were *less* descriptive.

So why not make her job in each situation sound directly relevant to customer service? We know she did a lot of customer service-type work;

why shouldn't she get credit for it? What you're aiming for here is *more* accuracy rather than less.

Now if you're experiencing a brain drain about how to apply this to your particular situation, I have three words for you: Use your imagination. In truth, I picked Liza as an example because it's a long stretch from receptionist to customer service. I wanted to show you that by using your imagination, and if at all possible the support of your current or previous boss, you can probably come up with something just like it that's both accurate and a portrayal of you in your DCD's light.

3. *List your schooling* in the third section of your resume, at the bottom of the page (and try to keep it to just one page). If you have a college or grad school degree of any kind, put that (them) down. If you've taken any relevant courses anywhere at all, list those too. A childcare worker who now wants to become a landscape designer, for example, might list educational experiences such as "Flora and Fauna, An Overview" at the Freetown Arboretum and "Gardening for Fun and Profit" at her hometown's Adult Education Center. *Anything* in your experience that relates directly to your DCD should go down here. Everything that's relevant builds your credibility. **NOTE**: If you have only a high school education and nothing else—no adult ed courses, no junior college certificates, no one-day workshops, nothing! —then just leave this entire section out… or go out and start earning such credits.

4. *Should you list dates?* That's a tough one. If you're working hard to build your career relationships and making some progress, this probably won't matter. Face-to-face, met with your fire and enthusiasm, most potential employers will tend to let the age question (whether "too old" or "too young") melt away.

If you're flying blind, however, spitting out your resume to employers unknown and unmet, you'll need to convey that you're not one who flits around from employer to employer at the drop of a hat. Yet some employers will think five years at one company is too long while others will think that's too few. So listing dates can be sort of a crapshoot.

That's why I run completely against the grain and suggest leaving dates out entirely. Why not? Let potential employers contact you with direct questions so as to discern your age, if that's what they care so much about. Of course that would also signal you that they have some interest in you. And that's when you turn on the ole dream career explorer charm and win them right over.

5. *Should you list your personal interests?* Sure…if they're relevant. A would-be landscape designer might list "rose garden, attending annual flower show, avid viewer of 'The Flower Shop' TV series on the HGTV channel." Amateurish? Vapid? Silly? Maybe, but when your qualifications are limited, you use whatever you've got, you pull out all the stops. To *not* mention these leisure interests and hobbies would be to imply you have no motivation for this job. Such omissions in fact *mislead* your resume readers by implying you don't have all that much enthusiasm, knowledge or experience when in fact you really do. So put *everything* in.

6. *How about job objective or summary of qualifications?* Nah. If you've structured the contents of your resume properly, employers will understand what you're looking for and why you're qualified for it. So just cut to the chase.

What do we have left to do for our brand spanking new success-style resume? All you've got to do now is:

- Cut down your "achievements" and "skills" section to manageable size. Cull irrelevant items from that long list I asked you to make back in step 1. Fit "talents" into whichever section seems most appropriate, or combine with "skills," i.e., "talents and skills."
- See that your achievements are not only relevant but also quantifiable, that is, with numbers included if possible. (Liza's resume does this well. Take another look at it.)
- Position what you deem to be the most impressive items on the top of your list.
- Add in headings.
- Use conservative, professional, standard fonts such as Times Roman or Arial, and not scripts or comic sands etc. Also, use only one font throughout, not a multiplicity of them.
- Print out a few copies of this grand masterpiece on quality bond paper to see how it looks while held in your hot little hands.
- Proofread! Proofread! Proofread!

Now then, my little career explorer buddy... you done got yourself one dang fancy resume.

What About Cover Letters?

Many human resources directors tell us they consider cover letters more an annoyance than anything else, brushing right past them on their way to the resume. This means your time will be better spent polishing the resume itself than your opening epistle.

But a cover letter of some sort is of course as much a necessity as a resume, so do craft one but keep it brief and to the point. Get through the niceties quickly and focus your second paragraph on what you most want your prospective employer to know about you. Then move on... don't make it a rehash of the resume or, worst of all, a tome!

Attention: John Spears, Director of Human Resources

Dear Mr. Spears,

I am attaching my resume for your consideration as regards your Customer Research Director position. You will see that I have a great deal of experience with projects aimed at better understanding how a company's customers are reacting to its products, including focus groups, surveys and committees. My interpersonal skills are exceptional and my ability to coordinate large projects has brought me praise.

My references are available upon request. If you would be willing to invite me in for an interview, I am certain you would not be disappointed.

Best regards,
Elizabeth Doolittle

CAREER TREASURE CHEST

Rachel's Assumption 4: **Job hunting is something you do alone.**

Flip Side: Always bring others along.

If you haven't adopted what I call a "careermate" by now, then get on with it! Traditionally people view a job hunt or career exploration as a solitary endeavor. Yet it must be obvious to you by now that I hold a distinctively different view. If I'm recommending the use of career allies, career relationships, mentors, and a personal board of mentors, I obviously firmly believe no one should be taking this lonely walk alone. And, good news here folks, many people in your life are willing *to take this walk with you!*

So what's a "careermate"? Basically, a career teammate, career colleague, career supporter and cheerleader, career best friend. This relationship often works best when your careermate is similarly engaged in a career transition at this moment, or has recently gone through one, because she'll thus understand what you're going through and want to help. But whatever his/her situation, I am certain you can find a careermate who will make a commitment to work with you so as to help you keep going. If your new careermate needs the same thing from you, you can make a commitment to reciprocate as well.

Be careful, however, exactly whom you choose. You'll need someone positive, creative, resourceful, and someone who cares about you. So ask yourself the following questions when considering careermate candidates:

- Is my potential careermate someone who has proven in the past to have my best interests at heart?
- Is my potential careermate someone who will push me when I need to be pushed?

- Does my potential careermate listen closely to me? Does he try to help me figure out what *I* want to do in my life, not what *he* thinks I should do?
- Is my potential careermate an optimistic personality who looks on the bright side of life and who believes we both can win?

If you can answer in the affirmative to most (or preferably all) of these questions, then sign him or her up! You'll want someone in this role who can really help you, and not just someone you like or who will take it easy on you. Sometimes you might need her to be tough. So think long and hard about your choice, then choose the winning candidate and take her out to a kickoff dinner! You're about to have lots of fun together.

Rachel's Assumption 5: **Rejection letters mean nobody wants you.**

Flip Side: Rejection letters mean nothing.

OK, you can *pretend* they mean something. You can take them personally, you can feel bad, you can tell yourself you're doomed.

But all they really mean is that you just haven't found your perfect match yet. It's out there, though. You just have to keep looking.

You might dramatically improve the odds, of course, by taking to heart what I've been saying in these pages all along: Rely more on building career relationships than on impersonal mailings of your resume. Rejection letters pile up only when career advancement plans emphasize those very traditional techniques that you know by now I heartily disdain.

Your likelihood of career-success-by-resume must be calculated in light of two somewhat disheartening factors:

1. Your competition is much, much greater within this venue, since most people take this road not the alternative paths I've been advocating.
2. If you have fewer face-to-face meetings, you will be judged primarily on inanimate paperwork, not on who you really are, what you can contribute and what you really *want*.

So stop shipping out so many darned resumes. Conduct your search for success amid oodles of real live people.

Advancement Tools Checklist

Let's now take stock of your advancement "tools." It doesn't hurt to have a career treasure chest well equipped with a toolbox and repair kit to supplement all the other ideas I've offered you. Remember, it always worked for Batman—just check out his utility belt!

In the list below, which items have you taken care to obtain or create?

- Resume
- Cover letter
- List of career allies, including contact info
- Carefully chosen careermate
- Board of mentors
- Membership in relevant professional organization(s)
- Contact with your alumni association
- Box of printed thank-you cards

How'd you do on this one? More and more these days, you hear about career advancement campaigns likened to the marketing plan of a business. That model demands making it easy for customers to understand the product (in this case, that's you) and being able to reach you when they want to. Thus with the first two items on this list, you're creating brochure and marketing materials, including the capacity to tailor these materials to your individual customers' (potential employers') needs.

We've already talked at length about the next four items on the list. We'd only add here that you should try to keep your career allies list as complete and up-to-date as possible, especially their emails. Any marketing expert worth her salt will tell you that your e-list or snail-mail list is typically worth ten times its weight in gold. Review it, revise it, work with it. Your coming career victory will likely emerge from it.

Have you forgotten about your alumni association? If you've graduated from a college, grad school, even your high school, each offers such resources. There might be a career library there too or free career counselors or at least an alumni directory available to you. So call them, check it all out. Visit your alma mater's website. Hey, they've been waiting to hear from you ever since you graduated!

Finally, there's the thank-you note. Do you always remember to send one? Sure, sure, we all say we will, and tell ourselves we really will... but then do you? If your answer is yes, then let me ask you this question: When was the last time you wrote out a thank-you and snail-mailed it off? Be honest now.

And here's a better one—when was the last time you *received* a thank-you note?

See our point? If everybody's running about mailing off so many thank-you notes to everyone else, then how come you and I don't receive all that many? Especially a handwritten one.

There are two schools of thought:

(1) Sending a formal thank-you might help if you want to spell out once again your most impressive career attributes and value contribution. This might make the most sense right after a job interview. Just be sure you've listened closely during the interview for what your potential employer wants most to find in his next hire. Then affirm in your thank-you letter whatever case you argued during your interview, i.e., that you're the one for the job!

(2) On the other hand, sometimes a handwritten note is the way to go. It can feel more genuine, more sincere, more demonstrative. Tom Peters in his *The Pursuit of* WOW! agrees with me: "Writing a note demonstrates a level of effort, and is permanent. Typed or handwritten? Handwritten by a country mile, a two-line, largely unreadable scrawl beats a page and a half spit out by a laser printer."

I line up with Tom. The more you make this game a personal one, the more likely you'll get exactly what you've come looking for.

DISCOVER **YOUR DREAM** CAREER

Legion of Career Heroes

JIM FAHEY: I Love the Ocean

Jim Fahey had found one of our early CareerScape exercises quite daunting: I had asked the class to complete a list of 100 "far-out dreams and ideas." Not career ideas or job titles necessarily, though those could be included too if they flowed naturally from the list-maker's imaginations. No, the true focus of this game was to simply let one's creative thinking flow, to see what spilled easily out, to fortify one's imagination, then to examine the resulting list and discern what it might say about them and what they want.

Jim had been the owner of a print shop, not a profession that encouraged a lot of departing from rote. Nonetheless, he had paid for our course and so he worked on his list dutifully. He wanted out of the print business, he knew that much but he had no clue whatsoever what career he might replace it with. So he gazed blankly out the window or at the white sheet of lined paper, racking his brain, and hoping to spot a trend or insight. Finally he lingered hopelessly at #1 on his list: "I love the ocean."

OK, so I love the ocean, Jim thought ... so what? How can *that* help me find a new career? Then, his next thought: Maybe I should just drive down to the ocean and see what I can find there? Maybe that's what my list is telling me to do.

Jim got in his car and drove a half-hour to the shoreline around Cape Cod Bay. Meandering up and down the country roads and stopping periodically to jot down a company's name, he ended up spending a couple of hours there, then drove back home and took a look at the new list he'd created. Hmmm, a dozen companies, none of which I have any idea about. What do any of them do?

Given this was way back in the days before the Internet, Jim could not Google the companies' websites. All he could do was pick up his phone and make some calls.

"Hello, my name is Jim Fahey," he would begin, typically speaking to a receptionist or switchboard operator. "I've been taking a career course lately and an exercise in the course has me thinking about how much I love the ocean. So earlier today I drove down to where your company is located and realized that I do not know what you do. Can you or someone else at the firm tell me? I really have no idea."

Well, an ancient CareerScape saying goes "Honesty is the best strategy," and Jim's totally hang-it-all-out-there honesty tended to bear this out. Each receptionist who had answered his call switched him to someone at her company who was willing to describe to him what that company did. Jim thus learned a fair amount about the companies he had encountered down by the bay.

One call however yielded much more than that. Upon being switched to one of the firm's principals, Jim found himself the recipient of a kind of royal treatment. The company co-owner was more than happy to chat with Jim at length, then, before hanging up, he invited Jim to come down again and meet him for a tour of the plant.

Jim smartly jumped at this opportunity and the next day enjoyed both a tour of the plant and a lengthy, in-depth career conversation with his new career friend Pete as well as lunch with Pete and his colleagues. At this lunch, Jim learned that this was an engineering firm that specialized in projects all around the world, like bridge projects, road projects, building construction and even scientific expeditions. The co-owners all generously shared details of all kinds with Jim, holding nothing back and offering advice to Jim on his career challenges as well as sharing stories about their own travails that got each of them to where they were that day.

In addition, Jim learned about specific problems and challenges this firm had been struggling with. Chief among these was a need to obtain government grant funding for a scientific expedition intended for Antarctica. All the way home, Jim wondered about this problem and the fact that his new friends at the firm had not had enough time to try to solve it. So instead of going right home, Jim headed to his local library (again, no Internet yet, remember) and attempted some research on the issue. After a few hours, he'd come up with some possible solutions.

The next day, Jim called Pete to share the solutions he'd come up with the day before. Impressed as all get-out with Jim's willingness to conduct such research on his own without having been asked, and intrigued by Jim's potential solutions, Pete invited Jim down to visit the company again, this time for a more formal meeting with Pete and his colleagues.

The punch line of the story? Jim visited the firm multiple times over the next few weeks, working (at no pay) with the firm's principals to come up with an effective solution to the grant-funding problem. Then, due in great part to his efforts, funding came through! Now the Antarctica project could move forward, finally, great news for this firm by the sea.

But, as well, this positive development created a brand-new challenge for the firm: Who would manage the project? All the company's co-owners and current managers were just too tied up with other projects to do so.

So they offered the job to Jim. Never mind that Jim was neither an engineer nor a corporate manager, though he had at least some ocean-going background, having served in the US Navy. And never mind that he had been running only a small print show for the past few years, not a major project or division in a major company.

Jim had simply placed himself in the right place at the right time, then demonstrated his value by showing the company's owners how easy he would be to work with and the kind of results he was capable of attaining.

"Had they put this new job out as a classified want-ad," Jim said later, "I would never have even gotten an interview. And they would have wanted someone with an engineering Ph.D! Instead they hired me without even asking to see my resume."

Jim's mere love of the ocean had started it all, then his many follow-up spontaneous steps kept it alive. He got hired for a job he was technically not especially qualified for. Yet the company chose to hire him because he showed them how much he cared about what they were doing and how very much he wanted to help them out.

8

MOVING ON UP

There's no guarantee that anything in this book will work. There's no way of knowing for sure that you will ever achieve any of your goals within the time you allot for them. Nor can you be certain that you will achieve any of them at all. Career advancement can sometimes seem like, or even actually become, a protracted battle that not everyone can win. Many in fact will give up.

Others will be disappointed with how things turn out. Still others will wage the very best, exceedingly most aggressive and effective campaigns imaginable… yet the chips will still refuse to fall where they should. As the great jazz bassist Russell George once said, "You have to remember: they don't *give* it away."

But you've got to try. Without conjuring up your hopes and dreams, without valiantly expressing them to the world, without embarking on an action plan to convert them into reality, nothing much will likely happen. You've simply got to fight for what you want. Sometimes you'll win and sometimes you'll lose. It's called "life."

I've found, though, that by putting goals down on paper, we can create a frame of mind that fires us to dynamic, practical action, a mysterious cause-and-effect dynamic that is not entirely explainable. But it does seem to work.

In fact, I have seen it work—we all have, really—exactly this way many times, not only in our own lives but in the lives of others, if only we look around us and acknowledge what we see. Again and again, I have observed in the ranks of my own clients and program graduates the astonishment of professionals who had managed to achieve a remarkably drastically different career change. Excitedly they would report to me that post-change they had taken a glance at career goals they had written out for themselves before getting started and were amazed to discover how very much of what they had recorded as mere hopes and dreams had now come true. Even for those who had stopped looking at their list of goals, stopped planning action steps, stopped reviewing their progress, they too apparently had created enough momentum to keep making the right things happen.

Your Career Advancement Action Planner

So let's set up this powerful but simple dynamic for you too. In the accompanying workspace, you may put together your very own structured career advancement action plan. You might also (instead) create an Excel grid (or similar) so that you'll be able to more easily revise it as you go along.

Feel free to modify this format, by the way, any way you'd like. It's just a good basic framework flexible enough to allow you to add other features that might better suit you. For example, some people like to leave spaces for "intermediate" career positions that would lead them to their eventual career destination.

Andrea, a middle school English teacher, decided she wanted to become a communications director one day at a major company. To get there, she targeted such intermediate steps as "communications intern," "communications assistant" and "communications specialist." She felt these positions would be logical sequences to prepare her for, and help her move ahead toward, her ultimate goal. So in her planner, she added spaces for these intermediate positions and then made room for "steps" and "resources" sections beneath each one.

Be flexible, too, about deadlines. Please see them as guidelines only. Understand that unforeseen circumstances often prevail over time intentions. If a deadline can't be met, just revise it! The point of all this action planning is to keep yourself going so you will ultimately get there, not necessary to get there "on time." Time is an artificial construct.

Dream Career Direction:
I'd like to achieve this by: [*Insert date*]

Now list 5-10 intermediate steps you'll need to take including deadline dates by which you should complete each:

Finally, list 3-5 resources that would help you achieve these steps and deadlines:

Some folks treat a goal or a deadline as a final report card on their commitment, their ability, or their self-worth. They go into a "shame spiral" if they don't do exactly what they said they'd do within a precise time frame they set for it.

When all is said and done, however, it probably won't matter one little whiff of a whit whether or not you attain your DCD in two years rather than in two-and-a-half. It's all so amazingly arbitrary. Just get yourself on that magical "belief track" that assures that yes you're gonna do it. Then slip into the driver's seat. The fact that you're doing all you can to get there is what really matters.

Building Career Relationships… Revisited!

Not long ago, Meghan, a savvy, aggressive former product-marketing manager, came to see me to ask my help with her current frustration. She'd been conducting her job search for six months and had hit a wall. She knew exactly what she wanted to find—a DCD in the consulting industry—and she'd been carrying out all her action steps, making lots of connections and steadily building her career relationships. "Yet," she lamented," I don't seem to be getting anywhere. I think I'm doing all the right things, but I'm not getting any job offers and not even interviews."

She showed me her career advancement planner and how she'd even added a section for relevant professional and personal information about each of her career allies. Over 600 names were in there, including addresses, phone numbers, emails, notes about personal interests (and foibles), plus sections with data on various targeted consulting firms, lists of all the major players—really, everything!

Meghan [*flipping through the pages, looking for a magic answer*]: What am I doing wrong? I'm meeting lots of people but nothing seems to be happening.

At first glance, Meghan did seem to be doing just as I'd advised her. But then I began asking her questions.

Me: Have you had career conversations with these people over the phone or in person?
Meghan: I speak to them first over the phone. Then if it seems to make sense I get them to meet me at their offices or over lunch. And yes, I pick up the check and mail them all thank-you notes.
Me: When do you follow up with them after that?
Meghan: I usually make a phone call about two or three weeks later to see if anything's come up since I last talked to them. If I don't get them in person, I leave a voice message for them. I don't want them to feel I'm pestering them.
Me: And when do you follow up with them after that?
Meghan: [*a little taken aback at this question*]: After that?

Me: Yes. After your second or third contact, when do you get in touch with them again?
Meghan: Well, I, uh, I don't.
Me: You don't? You stop talking with them?
Meghan: Well, as I said, I don't want to pester them. They've learned all they can about me, and they know what I'm looking for. After two or three contacts I figure they'll let me know if they hear of anything.

I reminded Meghan of Burger King, McDonald's and Wendy's pumping us with TV commercials every evening and billboards all up and down every highway. And don't forget Toyota, Cadillac, Hyundai, Ford and Jeep Wrangler. Or Sam Adams, Miller Lite, Budweiser, Coors and Heineken.

Me [laughing]: Why do you think all these companies keep "pestering" us so much?
Meghan [*seriously and without hesitation*]: Because they want our business! [*right now dawning*] Because each one wants us to think of them first!

The moral of my little recollection? While it's fine to take care that you don't become a pest, you must also take care not to stray over to the other side, the "gone-dark" side if you will, where you ensure that you are never heard from again. Those who advertise their wares to us ad nauseam do not wish to be forgotten. And they know that they will be if they hold themselves back. So keep advertising, reminding us, pestering—and never stop!

Backing me up here is Alan Weiss, one of the country's most successful management consultants, the very DCD Meghan was aiming for, who insisted in his classic, acclaimed how-to guide, *Million Dollar Consulting*: "It is actually difficult to contact clients too much. It is easy to fail to contact them frequently enough. The secret is simple: Establish an ongoing dialogue with clients. In the worst case, a monologue will do." To which Alan has since added (in his speeches and presentations): "If I don't toot my horn, I'll never hear any music."

So, as I explained to Meghan, by all means find ways to keep in touch, ways that are interesting, relevant, and nonthreatening, and keep them coming. If you don't, your contacts will definitely forget about you or, if they think about you at all, will believe they are no longer hearing from you because (a) you have given up your job search for whatever reason, or (b) you have found what you were looking for (and thus no longer need their help).

Tactics for Keeping in Touch

The next question for many of you will be: So how can I go about this? I certainly can't keep accumulating new names and contacts and call them all every week or take them all to lunch every month. Right, agreed, so true.

So here are a few tactical suggestions for keeping in touch:

- *Leave slightly chatty "thinking-of-you" voice mails.* Mention something relevant you heard in the news, or a good book you've just read that you think a contact would like, or maybe a link to an article. Don't make these voice messages too long though (90 seconds tops!) but just long enough to remind them you exist.

    You'll of course start off this way: "Just wanted to check in with you. I'm still out here searching for a position as a [*whatever*]. Please let me know if you get any ideas for me. Meanwhile I was thinking of you when I came across this book (or article or story etc.)…"

    End with "Anyway, you can still call me at [*phone number*] or email me at [*email*]. Thanks again for all your help so far. Bye for now."

- *Email your contacts a link to an article they might like.* Once you've had a good career conversation with someone, you'll then know a lot about them. Are they interested in fly-fishing? Management trends? Chaos theory? Lady Gaga? Samuel Beckett?

  Just email them something to read now and then with a message explaining, "Thought you might like to see this." Guess what? They probably will!

- *Periodically email "campaign updates."* These are kind of like ongoing status updates, which you're sending to people because you assume they want to know about your progress. After all, virtually all of them ended their first meeting with you with: "Let me know how you make out." So let them know already!

Item: "I'm still looking for contacts at Gerard Corporation. Anybody out there know anyone who works there? If so, thank you in advance."

Item: "I've gotten more familiar with leading customer service techniques in the retail industry. It's always fascinating to me to learn about customer service since that's what I want to do. Anybody know any good contacts in retail for me that I could have a career conversation with? Or any books or articles or websites for me to check out?"

It's like the board of mentors concept: You want to keep your career allies on your email list involved in your progress and you want them to be crystal-clear at all times about what you're looking for and how far along you are toward finding it. So be sure to ask them to email you back or call you if they should hear of anything. Put together a comprehensive email signature that includes your phone number, website or Facebook page, LinkedIn profile etc. Make it easy as pie to get back in touch with you. Never assume your career allies already know this stuff or have it close at hand.

Have You Hugged Yourself Today?

It's easy to forget to do, isn't it? Some of us don't even think we deserve it. Rarely does this question show up in a career or business book, or these three:

- Have you rewarded yourself today for taking on this challenge of career transition?
- Have you acknowledged yourself for how strong you are, how wise, how brave?
- Are you giving yourself the kudos you need to keep your spirits up and your confidence high?

Yes, this too is part of *your* current job, not just your careermate's. You've got to take time out now and then to smell the espresso. You've got to remind yourself why this battle is so important to you. You've got to credit yourself for taking on one of the hardest climbs in life—the excruciating baby-step-by-baby-step career hike to the stars.

You're halfway up the star ladder right now. Take a good look at the view. Look down (but hold onto the railings!). Look how far you have climbed. Congratulations!

Give yourself a hug.

Acknowledgment Mind Map

Time for another mind map? Let's label this one your "Acknowledgment Mind Map." This time you'll start it with "I Acknowledge Myself For" in the center and then proceed to do just that for all the tremendous personal progress you have made. Make your lines or tentacles represent "brave actions," "internal barriers broken," "new accomplishments," "lessons learned," and so forth.

When you run out of great things to say about yourself, show this map to your careermate or to a friend or spouse or co-worker or other career ally. Ask them to share what *they* think you've done that's so darned impressive. As always, have a lot of fun with this, use colored markers or crayons of course, and make it sparkle.

Taking Direct Action

No matter how hard you've worked or how much you've done (and accomplished), there often comes a point during this process when you feel as though you're hitting a wall. You *know* exactly which department, division, or new company you'd like to be hired by. You can see the perfect job title under your name. And, guess what, it's *not* the one you've labored under for the past 5, 10, 15 or 20 years.

When these kinds of visions begin pummeling you, the time has come for—trumpets please—Direct Action!

In some cases, Direct Action will be fairly straightforward. If you've decided to go back to school, you'll order a few college catalogues and begin poring over them. If you've decided to start your own business, you'll get some business counseling, perhaps secure a start-up loan and formulate a good business plan.

But if you've set your sights on a new employer-employee relationship, you've got to jump on any job leads you come across and generate as many new ones as you can. Remember, possibilities abound; you've just got to take the initiative to entice them your way.

Get started by examining your career allies list. Who's been good for you? Who's been a dud? Some on your list will be constantly feeding you great ideas, solid leads, encouragement and more. Place *A*'s next to those who have really helped you so far, *B*'s next to those who have only been OK, *C*'s next to those who haven't helped much at all. Has anybody been downright discouraging, antagonistic… stupid? Place a *D* next to this joker and cross him off your list. So long, fail-face!

Now ask yourself the following questions. Scan your allies list to jog your memory if answers don't come readily to mind.

- Have any of your allies mentioned current openings, or openings that may be coming up in the future?
- Have any of your allies mentioned expanding operations or new projects in their departments (or at their companies)?
- Has anyone commented on the need for someone new to come in and solve a festering problem?
- How might any of your allies benefit from adding you to their staff, perhaps in ways they're not even aware of?

Naturally you want to keep in mind your career vision. Not every opportunity or job opening is for you. You must continually ask yourself, "Is this something I want?" Be careful of jumping onto a bandwagon just because there's an opening of some kind. You don't want to land somewhere in a dream career direction that's not really in fact all that new.

When people have been at this process for a while, if nothing's yet come through, they sometimes begin getting fidgety. They start to think, "Maybe I ought to get practical and take something I know I can do for now. I can keep looking for my dream on the side. But maybe it's not yet my time."

Excuse my language but that's... bunkum! Your time is now. You're merely feeling your courage and self-confidence start to waver, which is natural considering all you've been through. So get back on your horse, cowpoke, and ride, ride, ride. Remember, there's gold in them thar hills!

Go now and take a second look at your career advancement planner, and at your career vision, and at all of your mind maps. You can do this, you really can. You can attain your DCD.

Getting in an Ally's Face

What can you say to your allies when you know they've got something you want? How do you talk turkey with them? How do you move this process along?

Elementary, my dear dream career hopeful: You level with them. You get together and you speak to them very directly. You ask them for exactly what you want. You call in favors. Like so:

> "Bill, as you know, I've been exploring a new career lately, and I've just completed a business course in risk analysis. The insurance field interests me more and more and I've learned a lot from you about your employer, People Mutual. So I've decided I'd love to work there. Are there any openings you know of? Is there anyone hiring you could help me meet?"

"Sarah, I've appreciated your help these past few months as I've explored my career options. I'm now certain that marketing is my future. What could I do to become a part of your department? I'd really be excited to work for you."

"Beth, I get more and more enthralled with everything I learn about the restaurant business. I've decided what I'd most like to do is manage. Do you know of any assistant management positions at any establishments in town? I realize you have nothing to offer me yourself right now, but anything you've heard of that might get me started would be great."

Don't try to copy down these speeches verbatim. They're designed just to give you the basic idea. You want to say what's on your mind in as natural a tone as possible, but you don't want to demand. You're just continuing to lead your allies in a way that helps you. You need something specific from them now, and you have to communicate that.

Taking this more direct approach now moves you into a more assertive phase in your climb toward your dream career. By now, if you've done your homework, you've established solid relationships in the new career area of your choice. Given that, you'll find many allies delighted that you're asking for help. Some may even have been wondering when you'd get around to it. Just remember that it's always your job to make known what you want, and to articulate to your allies how they can help you attain it.

The Dreaded Job Interview

Once you begin taking direct action, you'll also begin hearing about specific opportunities. At some point you'll advance to the formal step of job interviewing and doing whatever else it takes to capitalize on an opportunity.

But excuse me, ahem … did I hear you gasp a little when I mentioned interviewing? What's that you say? You'd rather wrap your hand around a red-hot fireplace poker? Oh, come on now, you can't be serious. The concept of job interviewing couldn't be that bad.

Yet of course for many (if not most) it very much is. The fear comes from worrying about getting it "right"—fielding tough interview questions, spitting back perfect answers, holding onto your cool while questions come flying at you left and right. It's like sharing tea and crumpets with an IRS auditor.

I'm not saying you don't have to prepare, or think through your answers, or phrase what you might say in terms that emphasize your strengths. It's just that, despite all of this, that indefinable connection, the potential chemistry between you and the interviewer, a mysterious "something" in the air, will have as much to do with any final decision as all of your "perfect" answers put together.

I'm forever asking audiences, for example, what criteria they've used in the past to hire someone when *they* have been on that side of the desk. I get essentially the same answers every time.

"It's a gut decision."
"Whether the candidate can fit in with the culture."
"How well I think we'll get along."
"Chemistry."
"The candidate's enthusiasm."

You've already convinced the interviewer that you're qualified, otherwise why would she have arranged this interview? Next, as with resumes, your interview should not throw your potential employer a curve ball. It should confirm everything the employer has come to believe about you up to now. If you just answer questions to the best of your ability, your store of knowledge, experience, and creativity should nestle you through.

But you can't fabricate chemistry. It's either going to be there or it's not. Because of this, you can't really "fail." If you generate enough job interviews, the right chemistry will materialize with someone. Your "perfect match" is out there waiting.

This natural chemistry is obviously what you most want to find. Otherwise, that new work environment with you in it won't be fun for anyone. Including you.

So my overall advice is this: The best job interview is a good career conversation. That's your guiding light. You want your interview, after all, to be, as Rick (Humphrey Bogart) suggests to Louis at the end of *Casablanca*, "the beginning of a beautiful friendship." You want it to assume the lofty position of a kind of supreme career relationship for at least the next few years. Think of it as the beginning of a long-running dialogue.

But next you may be thinking, incorrectly: "It's an interview and I'm not in control. My job is to shut up and answer the questions."

Well, it's true that we've been taught to think of interviews this way, yes, but that's not the surest path to success. Instead, put yourself in the catbird seat. Shift the process around so that it can serve your needs.

Interview Hint 1: Chat When You First Walk In

You'd be surprised how often employers report that this generally doesn't happen. People enter stiff, scared, subservient… not themselves.

In this state of mind, and behavior, you cannot hope to display the likeable, confident human presence that people who know you have come to appreciate about you in your current day-to-day life.

Break down these internal barriers! You're not back at your old job now, or at school taking a tough exam. You don't have to just shut up and follow orders. You're a grown-up! You're a real person, an entity all your own! So be friendly and informal right away, comment on the weather or the traffic or how nice a building this is or what interesting plants are on your interviewer's desk or how intriguing are her photos of family on the bookshelf. As long as you're not obnoxious, critical, or negative, it really doesn't matter what you actually say. You're just trying to break the ice and set the right tone that you've come as a potential new friend, you've come to interact and share … not just slavishly answer questions.

BUT NOTE: Don't let yourself be the only one chatting. While you'll want to chat a bit when you first come in, lord knows you don't want to run off at the mouth. Chatting is a two-way street: Let the person you're meeting slip in a few words as well. Watch where he goes with his comments, and follow the conversation wherever he takes it.

Also, anything you hear now could be a clue as to how this interviewer thinks, what she's looking for, how you could help this company. Keep chatting, but let your interviewer slowly begin doing more chatting, and more sharing, and more and more of whatever than you. Listen closely to what she has to say.

This bears repeating: *Listen closely!*

Interview Hint 2: Realize That Your Interviewer May Be Just as Nervous as You

Many interviewers, believe it or not, don't have the slightest idea how to conduct an interview. They fumble with your resume, they ask stilted, "textbook" questions, e.g., "So, uh, tell me about yourself" and "Uh, what is your greatest weakness?" and then they struggle to jot down your answers. Eccchhh! I could be outside playing Frisbee!

Ease your interviewer's mind, have pity on him. Subtly convert the interview into a career conversation. By helping your interviewer relax and enjoy himself, by the end of your session you'll have accomplished precisely what you came for. He will *like* you.

Interview Hint 3: Observe the "20/2 Rule"

When answering questions, keep them longer than twenty seconds but under two minutes. Too short and your answer will convey the impression that you the speaker have too little to offer. Too long your answer will evoke the image of a boorish windbag who lives only for the spotlight.

Even yes or no questions should be elaborated upon. Like other questions, they're opportunities to expand your case. Let's look first at the wrong way to do it, as exemplified by Candidate 1:

The Wrong Way

Interviewer: I see you went to Duke University.
Candidate 1: Yap.
Interviewer: Did you like it there?
Candidate 1: Yap.

Interviewer: You graduated with honors, third in your class—that's impressive.
Candidate 1: Yap, thanks.
Interviewer: Anything you'd like to add that we haven't covered?
Candidate 1: Nope.

Wow! What electricity, what excitement, what extraordinarity! You can literally picture your interviewer jumping up and down and shouting at the top of his lungs, "I so much love your simplicity! When can you start?" Yap, right.

Now compare that scenario with this unarguably vastly more effective one:

The Right Way

Interviewer: I see by your resume you went to Duke University.
Candidate 2: That I did. It wasn't my first choice back in high school, but it turned out to be the right place for me. I'd thought I'd prefer a smaller school closer to home—I'm from Wyoming—but as it turned out, the many opportunities at a major school afforded me, I believe, a richer and more diverse education.
Interviewer: So you ended up liking it there?
Candidate 2: Oh yes, very much so. I think that's where I first began enjoying scientific research, in fact. Though I studied a straight business curriculum, they always had major science exhibits going on there, and I became fascinated by them. That's why this position as a scientific research assistant appeals to me so much. I've become very drawn to science.
Interviewer: I see too that you graduated with honors, third in your class. *Impressive.*
Candidate 2: Thank you. I studied pretty hard there. I always felt my education was an opportunity to grow, not just pick up a diploma.

So I threw myself into it. I took my commitment to my workload pretty seriously, hard as it was at times.

What do you think? Whom would you prefer—Candidate 1 or Candidate 2? Obviously, by adding her charm and responsiveness to her impressive credentials, Candidate 2 clearly wins the game. Elaborating upon what could have been simple yes (yap) or no answers, she identifies herself as (1) curious and eager to learn, (2) interested specifically in scientific research, and (3) a very hard and willing worker. Not a bad set of attributes for the new hire that you want to fill this job.

Interview Hint 4: Ask Questions

Interviews, by definition, tend to be one-sided. One person (job interviewer, reporter, pollster) asks questions of another, and then the other responds. That's pretty much the way it's supposed to go. And that's one reason I disdain informational interviews.

But a conversation works differently, doesn't it? Both parties ask questions, both answer questions, both make expansive comments. There's a give-and-take, there's an equal exchange. A relationship forms.

You want to create that here—a career conversation. That means you've got to throw in some questions of your own. On a very, very discreet level, you've got to alter the format.

Here's how you do it: Sometime after the interview gets started—maybe five or ten minutes, probably no longer than fifteen (trust your instinct)—slip in a few questions at the end of one of your answers. Make this question as spontaneous as you can. Let it spring from something that's come up during the interview. For example:

Interviewer: Tell me, Melissa, what makes you feel especially qualified for this position of scientific research assistant?
Melissa: Well, I'm a pretty organized person and I can see that you'd have to be organized to keep all these research data points in order. Which brings up a question I wanted to ask you: How closely would I be involved in the actual experiments themselves? I'd love to work directly in the lab at some point. Would that be a fit with this position?

Notice how Melissa slides the question into the interview naturally. It is an honest thing to ask, after all, and it's worth asking simply to understand more about how things work around here. It also communicates clearly where Melissa wants to go in her professional development should she be invited to work here.

Now the interview can move in a whole new direction, becoming more and more a genuine conversation. If the interviewer spends even a few minutes responding to Melissa's question, a tone has been set that allows for a free-flowing give-and-take. They begin a career conversation, and as a result, a potentially long-term career relationship.

Interview Hint 5: Paint the Future, Not the Past

When making a case for yourself, don't dwell on jobs, functions and achievements in your past. Explain how transferable your demonstrated skills and your accomplishments can be to a new situation. You will most effectively make the transition to your DCD if you literally "see" yourself working there. That means picturing yourself employing talents, skills, and abilities in the service of your new career. Once you've got that in your sights, all you need next is to describe it for someone who can help.

Is This a Better Deal?

A day will come when you finally get a job offer that's not what you're doing now. It really will. So go ahead and shout "Glory hallelujah! Someone wants me, someone wants me!"

At that moment, though, you will face a brand new question: Should you take it?

Go back to your career vision. Does this offer *really* represent what you've been looking for? Is it the right job for you? How's the compensation look, and the benefits? Will this position take you anywhere?

Give yourself a day or two to think about it. No matter how much you may want a new situation, it's always a good policy to sleep on it. You might be missing something, forgetting something. If you are, it could hit you like a ton of bricks 24-48 hours later.

When you do call them back in the next day or two, be diplomatic, courteous, respectful, enthusiastic, positive. But ask as well for something more. Maybe it's more money, or a longer vacation, or an upgrading of authority or responsibility. The worst they can tell you is, "We can't do that." At least you'll have tried. Most times you'll win on at least a few points.

But now you may be thinking: Ugh, I hate playing games. I'm just not comfortable with that. I just want this new job.

Well, it's already a game. Your potential employer more than likely expects you to come back with a request for more, they've probably factored that in. "If she asks for $2,000 more a year, let's offer her $750," they may have agreed behind their closed doors. "If she won't accept that, we'll go to $1,000, maybe $1,200. But $1,400 is our ceiling." That's how this game is often played.

If you refuse, however, to play any games at all, your discomfort may cost you a lot of money. Or more time off. Or a job level more to your liking. Or this or that.

So at least play a *little* game.

How do you ask without alienating everybody? Just be careful with your language. Don't say, "You gotta gimme this. It's mine and I deserve it." Be diplomatic instead: "What could we do to make this work for both of us? Your figure of $34,000 feels a little low to me. I was really hoping for $40,000. What can we do to get closer to that amount?"

At some point, after playing around with the areas you'd like to see "improved," you'll get a feeling in your gut that it's time to say yes. When that moment comes, tell your new employer you're glad to be aboard. "I think we're all set," you say. "I feel great about our agreement. I'm looking forward to working with you."

Yahoo! Pop the cork on some Dom Perignon. You've just made your new employer happy. And you've freed yourself from the dregs of your job search and the shackles of your current old-career or non-career situation.

Legion of Career Heroes
RICK DeANGELO: Corporate Volunteer

Conventional career wisdom has always had it that volunteering one's time for, say, a nonprofit group or a professional association, in order to make contacts, build career relationships and hear about job leads, is a worthy investment of one's time. But other than serving as an unpaid internship at a for-profit company, who among us has ever considered "volunteering" for such an organization, and a Fortune 500 one at that?

"Big companies have so much money, why would I ever do that?" goes the typical thinking. "Hey, a for-profit company should be PAYING me to work for them!"

Yes, possibly true, except that if they don't understand your potential value to them, or for that matter if they have never met you, why would they? So instead we typically jam ourselves into intense competition with hoards of other wannabees who all submit their resumes for the very same (and very few) paid formal job slots being offered. Who's going to pay you for doing *that*?

When you think creatively about something though, you sometimes come to a different conclusion, in this case that getting a big, fat, high-profit company to get to know you and to see what you can do just might be the ticket to causing them to *want* you, and to be willing to pay you to come work for them. Might not that be worth any short-term work freebie you might donate to them?

Rick DeAngelo looked at things this very way one day while engaging in a career conversation at Anheuser-Busch. Though equipped with a bachelor's degree in business and an accounting position at the prestigious Big 8 accounting firm of Peat Marwick (his first job out of college!), Rick had more and more felt himself coming to a career dead end. After 18 months at Peat Marwick, Rick just couldn't take it anymore, longing to get away from the endlessly left-brain mind melt of numbers, numbers, numbers. He ached to do something *fun* and RIGHT-brained.

During his CareerScape sessions, he recalled a summer when he and a friend had put together a line of T-shirts which they marketed successfully to tourists on Martha's Vineyard. They didn't get rich from the endeavor but Rick remembered it as at once fun and stimulating. Challenging of course too but in a positive way. He wished he could get that feeling back again.

Once this insight hit him, he knew that getting out of accounting was unavoidable. For the sake of his sanity, heading in a direction like marketing made far more sense. So one day he found himself sitting in the office of an executive at Anheuser-Bush, having gotten there via the connection of a mutual career ally, and asking lots of questions about the company's marketing efforts and future. The exec was as helpful as could be but of course knew of no internal job openings to send Rick to at that moment. "But I'll send your resume over to HR," he offered genially, "and maybe something will come up."

Walking Rick to the door of his office to say goodbye, Rick all of a sudden felt a light bulb go on. "One last thing," he said. "Would there be any possibility of *volunteering* for the marketing department or some other part of the company?" he asked. "Volunteering. No pay."

Taken somewhat aback, the exec stopped for a second, then stammered, "Well, no, not volunteering, I don't think so. Probably not." Then all of a sudden his own light bulb went off! "You know, there are a few lower-level jobs available in our merchandising department," he thought aloud. "Hmmm, maybe you'd want one of those?"

The executive then outlined what he knew of these "lower-level" jobs: Merchandising, basically a segment of Anheuser-Busch's Marketing division, was nonetheless an integral cog in the Marketing "wheel." Though the job paid only minimum wage and mostly involved driving a company van to stores and restaurants and bars to drop off product samples (new beers, wines, bar nuts) and advertising posters and cardboard displays, the position was kind of like a Marketing bottom rung.

So Rick listened and counted the opportunities: a chance to get inside this mega-company's doors, a chance to prove what he could do on the ground floor, a chance to rub shoulders with folks in Marketing itself… etc. He would gradually become a colleague of those on the inside, not a faceless hopeful jostling within a massive crowd of applicants on the outside.

Rick took the job, did it well for about six months, then heard about an opening in Marketing, which he applied for and got. Within a few years he had moved over to a high-level marketing position at a biotech firm nearby, leaving a few years after that to found a Massachusetts-based retail business with his wife Lesley called Vows which sells high-quality wedding dresses at deeply discounted prices to budding brides. Their new service which they still run today brought Rick full circle from those youthful eager days on Martha's Vineyard when a modest line of T-shirts had offered him the fun and stimulation of entrepreneurship, a business life that still fulfills all his dream career criteria.

9

HOW SOCIAL MEDIA CAN HELP (AND HURT)

One summer, one of my star interns Maggie Sutherland came into my office with a suggestion she felt very strongly about. "We should put the company on Twitter," she said, to which I astutely replied, "Excuse me?"

"Twitter. It'll help you communicate better with our clients."

Once more, my response was precisely calibrated: "Tweeter? Twitt-what? I don't have any idea what you are saying."

Maggie then eloquently explained to me what Twitter was and how it worked and why it could be so important to my business. I listened carefully, hanging on every word. When she had finished, I was still without a clue.

I authorized Maggie to go ahead and set up Twitter that day calculating that once she had, maybe then I would understand what it was all about. But even once that happened, I still could not fathom how this would reach our clients or why it should supplant (or replace) email.

A few weeks later I was in a convenience store one weekday afternoon and roaming the aisles as a TV set up in a corner of the store blared a human interest feature from CNN. The story concerned a poor chap (we'll call him Mel) who had gotten laid off recently from his professional job and had begun the traditional next-step of updating his resume, researching companies he might like to work for, and applying for relevant job openings.

But Mel's story was unique in that, from the moment he was called into his boss's office and told, due to the company's downsizing, that he was now, officially, no longer employed, he didn't simply mope around and get depressed but began recording every occurrence and emotional reaction in real time and tweeting them out to his small band of followers.

This meant, to the best of his ability, *everything*: the boss's very words, his inner shock, his confusion over how this could happen, the sad task of cleaning out his office, his attempt to get through the rest of the day, the reaction of his wife, his growing anger that this could happen, the sober struggle of trying to explain this "transition" on his resume ... everything.

What's more Mel continued to tweet each development obsessively as the days and weeks wore on. His tweets averaged one a minute!

The kicker to the story was that, after a few weeks of this, his follower numbers grew, as did re-tweets of his difficulties and, therefore, even more followers. Direct messages poured in too, from followers commiserating after experiencing the same thing, to followers telling him to

HOW SOCIAL MEDIA CAN HELP (AND HURT)

"keep his chin up," to successful job hunters offering him advice, to … and this is what *really* got my attention … people passing along actual job leads to him or influential contacts who might be able to help. In essence, tweeting what had happened to him, moment to moment, action by action, thought to thought, emotion by emotion, literally became his job search. Camped out at his laptop, pouring out his heart and day-to-day challenges, he replicated what the age-old low-tech job search campaign professed to do: locate job openings, job interviews and job offers.

This last of course was the Golden Fleece, an actual job *offer* or two. In that, the CNN report didn't let me down either. During the course of his Twitter adventure, over perhaps 3 or 4 weeks, Mel also received TWO actual job offers, from employers he had never met, only communicated with via social media. Now I could finally understand what Twitter might be all about: a real-time communication system that can bring people together who valued each other in the marketplace, or perhaps simply valued each other for personal reasons, e.g., similar recreational interests, help with one of life's mysteries (romantic relationships, parenting, career issues) or a similar taste in movies, sports or music.

A year or so later, I would see this last scenario play itself out when my daughter Chloe, in high school at the time, began tweeting steadily with a half-dozen or so girls approximately her own age about music they all loved. At some point, Chloe tweeted she had started doing a program twice a month for her high school radio station, focusing of course on the same category of music that had brought them all together. Before long, many of her Twitter friends were taking time to listen to Chloe's program as it streamed over the Internet, even though her social media friends were located half a continent away and in one case half a *world* away. Though Chloe's program emanated from a tiny, tiny broadcast signal in Massachusetts, her listeners' locales extended to Minnesota, Arizona, California ... and Croatia!

Predictions a Bust

Once Maggie set Twitter up for me, and as I began to understand what it was, how it worked and what it could do, I authorized Maggie and my other interns to set up other social media accounts, chiefly LinkedIn and Facebook. The rise of social media, and the clamor of businesses to get involved with it, in fact began steamrolling so fast that by the end of that summer, I was already way behind the curve. But I tried to listen intently to the predictions of social media advocates: businesses *must* get involved, business communication is definitely headed for a major transformation, businesses and individual professionals and experts within the next year or so will simply not be able to get along without these new vehicles.

I have to say however that, in my view, such predictions have never quite come true. Not that we can't cite a few industries or professions here and there that rightly claim it has helped them function far more effectively (PR reps, many sales reps and the entertainment industry). But for the vast majority of professionals, the predictions have been quite a bust. Nowhere is this truer than in the realm of career change and job hunting. Ironic of course given my first insight into social media manifested itself in Mel's successful job hunt.

Take my research for this chapter, for example. In all these years since hearing that CNN report about Mel, I've not encountered any similar tales nor rarely heard of a friend or relative or acquaintance for whom social media played the majority role in a successful job search. Oh I know they happen, of course, because, distantly, I have occasionally heard of someone who claims to have "gotten" his or her job via

HOW SOCIAL MEDIA CAN HELP (AND HURT)

social media. But the stories are always fuzzy, skimpy, tangential. Other than good ole Mel, I have never since heard of anyone getting a job offer via LinkedIn or Twitter or Facebook without some more traditional behavior (networking, career conversations, answering an ad) playing the more significant part.

So, to be fair, I decided to test my bias against the experiences of others and see if I could come up with a number of stories of successful social media job campaigns to use in this chapter. To unearth such results, it seemed only logical to utilize social media itself for this research. So I decided to poll my LinkedIn connections and ask them if they, or someone they knew, had ever obtained a job via social media or at least successfully utilized social media as a job search or career change tool.

Results of this social media missive, I must confess, were not stupendous. Within the next few days I received about a half dozen responses, all of them to this effect: "Hi Ken, I don't have any stories for you but it's nice to hear from you. Hope you're doing well!" After a couple of weeks, I did receive a message from Pete, a connection in Dallas who told me he had a friend who had been successful finding a job through LinkedIn, and then set up an email introduction for us. However, Pete's friend never got in touch with me so I remain uninformed about his story.

Because my LI inquiry had met with such barren results, I decided to try another approach, though not via social media this time. Instead I used a daily inquiry service for journalists called Profnet that introduces writers and editors working on stories or books to potential interviewees, enabling them to recommend themselves as sources in a certain subject matter. So I placed such a call-for-help inquiry in the form of the simple request I'd used in LinkedIn, that is, has anyone out there ever obtained a job via social media or perhaps successfully utilized social media as a job search or career change tool?

Since Profnet goes out to thousands of upon thousands of subscribers multiple times per day, I expected a much stronger response than from LI. I mean, how could it *not* be stronger? I had nowhere to go but UP!

After a few days, I had received only one response:

Hi Ken,

I saw your Profnet looking for instances where social media helped a career change. For me, I was already in the world of PR, but my career change was still substantial. I had previously worked in-house (not for an agency) and I had no experience with financial firms prior to being hired to work exclusively with financial clients.

I found a recruiter in a Facebook group, reached out to her, we met for coffee after a long phone conversation, and she immediately felt I'd be a perfect fit for this company. A few months in I can say that I certainly agree – and that it's a career I never would have considered had she not convinced me.

Best, Caitlin Byrnes, Social Media Specialist

What surprised me of course was that even through this more conventional process, i.e., email, hardly any experiences were being offered. Didn't the mere law of averages suggest that there might be 5, 10, maybe even 15 successful social media job hunters out there who would be

HOW SOCIAL MEDIA CAN HELP (AND HURT)

overjoyed at the prospect of spreading the good word about this revolutionary new approach that they themselves had found?

OK, OK… well how about just more than *one*?

I next tried more orthodox research, over the Internet, just good old faithful Googling. I tried such keywords and phrases as "social media job hunting," "social media career search," "social media success stories career change" etc.

The result this time was a plentitude of articles about how social media can help in a job search, top ten lists for doing so, advice from career and/or social media experts, and so on. There is even a category of article on what *not* to do, i.e., dangers and pitfalls.

Upon examination of all of these articles however, I found that virtually none of them included *examples* of social media job hunt success. Even on websites like Monster.com and CareerBuilder, I could find neither customer examples nor case studies. Maybe they were there on those premier sites but if so, I couldn't easily find them. You would think such illustrated testimonials would be prominent if they in fact existed.

Hmmm, this was very concerning. While these articles did claim that social media "obviously" helps one find a new job, concrete case studies were few and far between. 99% of the time, they were not visible at all!

What could I conclude from all of this? Well, gee willikers … what would *you* conclude?

It struck me that although anything in life is possible, social media by and large is not going to actually "get" anyone a job. That initial

Twitter story I'd heard on CNN way, way back had to be an anomaly. Hey, that's why they call it *news*, kids!

But then again, that could be said for a resume too, could it not? No employer is going to review a resume and then just say, "OK, I am convinced, I am going to hire this person." Nope. Instead, one's resume can get you in the door, a la: "OK, I am convinced. I am going to interview this person." And a great resume will get you through a *great* door but once through your personal interaction and persona and ability to communicate your value and expertise will be responsible for taking you to the goalpost. Likewise, this same scenario can occur with the help of social media.

So, in that light, let me share with you what seem like sensible insights from one particular Internet article that I came across as I scoured the web for an understanding of social media's value as a tool for discovering and attaining your dream career. None of them will win you a job per se. But all of them can help move you along toward that great door you want to get yourself through:

PLEASE NOTE: The excerpts below have all been harvested from an article written by Jacquelyn Smith, a staff writer for Forbes Magazine in its April 16, 2013 issue.

"CareerBuilder (has) found that 37% of employers use social networks to screen potential job candidates. That means about two in five companies browse your social media profiles to evaluate your character and personality–and some even base their hiring decision on what they find."

"A third (34%) of employers who scan social media profiles said they have found content that has caused them not to hire the candidate.

HOW SOCIAL MEDIA CAN HELP (AND HURT)

About half of those employers said they didn't offer a job candidate the position because of provocative or inappropriate photos and information posted on his or her profile; while 45% said they chose not to hire someone because of evidence of drinking and/or drug use on his or her social profiles. Other reasons they decided not to offer the job: the candidate's profile displayed poor communication skills, he or she bad mouthed previous employers, made discriminatory comments related to race, gender, or religion, or lied about qualifications.

(So) ... "(m)ake sure any profiles you write are free of typos, the information is coherent and applicable to your industry [or job you're trying to land], and your photos present you in a favorable light. You can verify the applicability of the information by checking profiles of others in the same field."
—Brad Schepp, co-author of *How To Find A Job On LinkedIn, Facebook, Twitter and Google+*

"The good news is that hiring managers aren't just screening your social media profiles to dig up dirt; they're also looking for information that could possibly give you an advantage. The CareerBuilder survey revealed that 29% of surveyed hiring managers found something positive on a profile that drove them to offer the candidate a job."

"This means job seekers shouldn't just focus on hiding or removing inappropriate content; they should work on building strong social networks and creating online profiles that do a really good job of representing their skills and experience in the workplace."

(Thus) ... "(i)t's not enough to only post a profile and check your news feed. There are a lot of lurkers–people who have an online profile but don't do anything or engage in any meaningful way. You need to give to the social networking communities, participate in group discussions, share expertise, point someone to an article. You have to work it. While it can feel uncomfortable putting yourself out there, if you're looking for a job, it's not the time to be timid."

10

SETTLING INTO NEW DIGS

So here you are, at your new desk in your new office in that new building. Your window looks out on the breathtaking cityscape below, and you even have a door you can close. You've got the service of an assistant to help you out, though maybe you share him with three others... but that's all right.

Or maybe it's just a gray-walled cubicle. But it's *your* cubicle, and they are paying you to dwell inside it. Get to work fixing up your workspace the way you like: a little vase with flowers that you picked up on the way to work today, a few small pictures of your loved ones, your favorite paperweight, that cute, tiny little desk calendar. As you fuss about, smile to yourself and say, "I've worked very hard to get here. I deserve to feel good."

Give yourself such a moment.

Nurturing a New Professional Self-Image

Next question: Do you really see yourself yet as a professional on the level of this new exciting position? Can you really see it, feel it? Can you really believe it?

If you're having trouble with any of this, create a pack of what I'll call "New You Cards." Get a stack of index cards and deal out about fifteen or twenty. On each card, write out a statement that expresses something about the New You. Make each statement affirmative, active, dynamic. Also, make it something you haven't quite grasped yet, that you're not yet sure you truly believe.

But above all, make it something you absolutely *want* to believe.

Once you've put together your New You Cards, keep them with you all day long. From time to time yank them out and shuffle through them reading each carefully, sensing how strongly (or how little) you believe what each card says.

At first, you'll not sense a real connection with any of the cards. You'll feel as though they're talking about someone else. But remember this: They're designed to help you acquire a *new* image, not to reinforce the one you already have. They're describing a you that is in-the-making.

As you read through your cards time after time after time, day after day, you'll begin reprogramming your mind. Some of the cards' statements will begin getting inside of you. They'll work their subtle magic on your internal barriers, so that one day you'll pick up a card, read it, then matter-of-factly think, "Well, yes, that's true." Once that happens… throw the card out! Then replace it with a new one. This new card's statement will now express another belief about yourself that you haven't adopted or accepted yet.

It's important to see your DCD position as a step forward for your new self, and to begin discarding, or at least taking control of, old beliefs that no longer serve you. As the title of Peter McWilliam's book states,

You Can't Afford the Luxury of a Negative Thought. Understand that, and get in the habit of positive thinking.

Tooting Your Own Horn

You've apparently been doing this pretty well. After all, it was central to your career advancement campaign, which of course has gotten you this far. And though advertising yourself may not have been the most comfortable fit at first, I am quite certain that by now you've gotten the hang of it, or at least a little more used to it. In your DCD work environment, however, you've got to take it up a thousand notches.

See all those busy beavers scurrying around outside your new office space? How many of them have you gotten to know yet? I don't mean by that you've been casually introduced. What I mean is: how many have you *really* gotten to know?

That's precisely what you have to do next. You can't just wait for people to approach you—that's old-time career world stuff. This time around you must approach people before waiting for them to approach you. You want them to think of you as a true team player and you want to assure them you are here to make a real difference to your new workplace "family."

So invite each of them to have lunch with you sometime. (And yes, you will still lunge for that tab!) In the process of getting to know them, you're continuing your career advancement by initiating career conversations and building and deepening your new career relationships.

Seeking Out Feedback

In your new career life, you'll also want to seek out feedback, especially if you never did so before. And what's more, this time you'll relish it.

That's right, you'll look for it, seek it out, uncover it, ask that it be delivered right to your door. In this new position you can't afford to let your mistakes go uncorrected or your bad habits fester. You need to be on top of things. You need to succeed, without reservation.

How can you be sure that you develop steadily this time, that you grow professionally, and that you incorporate "unsuccessful experiments" (failures, mistakes, errors) into a learning curve that makes you better? HR expert Paul Falcone has said that asking your new boss for periodic performance reviews throughout the year would be one way to go about it. As he has written:

> By asking your boss for quarterly or even monthly performance updates, you'll show yourself as someone looking for ways to improve [her]self, an individual open to constructive criticism, and a person with outstanding communication skills. Most significantly, you'll get a steady stream of feedback that will help you improve your performance. That way, when it comes time for the annual performance appraisal, you'll have had a head start on gathering the information necessary to have fixed most of the weaker issues in advance! This is a winning strategy for a well-informed, career-conscious, information-hungry employee geared for career progression.

Wise words: Speak to your new boss about conducting frequent performance reviews today.

Piping Up at Staff Meetings

Maybe you did a lot of this at your last place of work or as a student in class, although many folks admit they really didn't contribute much out loud unless they had to. But this time, because you've now embarked on a major step toward fulfilling your dream career, it's time to behave differently.

So speak up! Say your piece. Inject an idea or a question into the fray here and there. Let people hear what's on your mind. Talk!

It's a good idea, however, to *listen* too, especially in your first few weeks. Make sure not to chime in too fast with too many of your fabulous new opinions and ideas. People will accept you more readily if, in the early days, you don't act like you know it all before you've had much of a chance to know *anything*.

So yes, contribute a bit so that people start to recognize you and give you some props, but also bide your time a bit too. Take a lot in, hear people out, ask questions about references you don't understand or terminology that's new. Observe the group dynamics in your new department or at company staff meetings so you've got a pretty good sense of the lay of the land. See to it that you position yourself as a player, a minor one at first but then a major one. You've been hired to be fully involved, eventually. So get on your way.

NOTE OF CAUTION: For your new relationships to gel effectively you must negotiate and discover some common ground. That will happen best when you have taken time to genuinely listen to others and absorb what they are saying. Absorb, mull, process and understand. And always keep listening. Smells like team spirit.

Setting Boundaries

In your previous situation, you may not have always felt comfortable saying no to your boss when he'd dump a piping hot stack of documents on your desk at ten minutes to five and then mutter gruffly, "I'll need these translated into PPT slides by eight tomorrow morning." Then (almost forgetting): "Have a nice night."

You may never have set boundaries around how much work or what the work itself might be that could be agreed as reasonable vs. unreasonable. Or how much over each line would be A-OK.

So if you've never learned to set limits before, maybe now would be a jolly good time to start. If you don't, you'll slowly revert to your previous ways all over again. You're likely working in a fast-paced pressure-cooker environment this time around and you want to be ready when people wander by to take advantage. Of course they may be taking advantage without even realizing it, but "take advantage" is still "take advantage" nonetheless. That's why it's up to you to set boundaries. No one else will step in and do it for you.

The following scenarios suggest stepping-over-the-boundaries dilemmas you might find yourself faced with in your new dream position. Think for a moment how you should handle any of these situations should they come storming your way.

SETTLING INTO NEW DIGS

DILEMMA 1

One of Belinda's new colleagues, John, asks her to take over a "minor" project he's been having trouble with. "You know a lot more about this than I do, Belinda," he says. "Maybe you could work it through for me?"

Belinda knows she's got a lot on her plate right now. How can she tactfully deflect John's request? Make a few notes here summarizing your thoughts:

_____

_____

_____

_____

_____

DILEMMA 2

Mark's boss Hermione drops a weighty assignment into his in-basket. She's marked it ASAP on a post-it and Mark recalls this same problem, time and time again, at his previous job. In fact, he's already rushing to finish another assignment Hermione had given him, due by the end of this week.

So which is more important? How can Mark know what Hermione truly needs first (or most) and how much priority he should ascribe to each? Make a few notes here summarizing your thoughts:

_____

_____

DILEMMA 3

Marguerite's new boss, Mr. Hightower, invites her and her husband, Jim, to dinner on Saturday night at his house. But it's the third time in the last two months, and Marguerite has begun to feel enough is enough. Jim's not too pleased either.

What should she tell Mr. Hightower? Make a few notes here summarizing your thoughts:

DILEMMA 4

Some new colleagues of Lisa's meet every Thursday for lunch. Lisa quickly sees that all that ever seems to go on at these luncheons is office gossip, snippy comments, and cynical remarks.

Lisa's joined them three times already but doesn't want to continue. What can she do or say to get out of this one? Make a few notes here summarizing your thoughts:

SETTLING INTO NEW DIGS

_____

_____

_____

_____

_____

There are an infinite number of responses that any of us could come up with for any of these scenarios so don't look at your answers as a right-wrong thing. Whatever works, especially in touchy situations, can be deemed correct.

But the main thing is that all your responses should be based on an essential need for you to remain sensitive, tactful and respectful. You don't want to start alienating the same folks you're trying to win over. Don't get angry, get resourceful. Choose your words and reactions with care, then launch into them. Here are some responses I feel meet such criteria:

Response to Dilemma 1: "I'd like to help, John, I really would, but honestly I can't fit anything new in right now." Belinda thinks a moment. "But what I could do is take a few minutes and help you figure out how you could best handle this. I do have a little more experience here, so maybe I can act as your 'consultant.' Why don't we sit down at lunchtime and talk about steps you could take to get you through this."

Response to Dilemma 2: Mark should ask for guidelines straight out. "I can get right on this new assignment, if that's what you want," Mark tells Hermione. "But I have a question for you: Should I drop this other assignment I've been working on? When you say ASAP, when exactly do you mean? What's your absolute deadline for each of these assignments?"

Response to Dilemma 3: "Mr. Hightower, would you mind if Jim and I passed on your kind invitation this Saturday? We've enjoyed dinner with you and Mrs. Hightower in the past, but lately we feel we haven't been spending as much time at home as we'd like. For the time being, we've decided to cut down on our social events and just spend more time with each other."

Additional advice: If Mr. Hightower doesn't take the hint and his invitations persist, then a heart-to-heart talk may be in order. Is Mr. Hightower the kind of person an employee can talk to frankly? If so, Marguerite should tell him that, in her experience, when boundaries between work and personal life get too ambiguous, they make relationships at work confusing and ambiguous too. Bosses may start having trouble telling their "employee friends" what to do; employees have trouble allowing their "boss-friend" sufficient authority. Maybe there's an experience from Marguerite's past or an experience of a friend of hers she could relate to Mr. Hightower.

In any event, this approach, when it works, will also avoid future cat-and-mouse games with an overly chummy boss. It takes a little more courage to raise an issue like this face-to-face, but the payoff could be longer lasting.

Response to Dilemma 4: Lisa should put her colleagues off by eating lunch at her desk, or saying, "I have so much to do, I'm working through lunch today." She should also start making plans to meet other folks for lunch. Though her "old buddies" may start gossiping about her, once she begins avoiding them, at least she'll be free.

Additional advice to Lisa: Don't waste a moment of your precious workday on things that won't advance you, or that are petty or mean-spirited. Get away from those folks as fast as your little legs can carry you. That's right, you heard me: *Run!*

Sliding Back Down the Big Chute

You don't want to unconsciously step onto a trapdoor and drop back down to where you came from. You don't want to feel like you're going backwards.

SETTLING INTO NEW DIGS

Keeping yourself from sliding back down the big chute that you've just baby-stepped your way out of may require summoning lots of stamina. You'll also need to stay alert and in shape. So here are two tips to maintain your "career fitness":

1. *Don't be afraid of seeming stupid.* You have to ask questions. You have to admit you're in the dark about a lot of things. You have to fully understand your new projects and assignments. You have to get any and all new procedures explained clearly to you.

    When you pretend to be too "smart," you may end up failing to learn what you need to know. Listen to your colleagues and hear what they're saying. When you don't understand something, ask them to explain it again. You might take a colleague aside and ask him to explain it at a later time rather than take time at a staff meeting and risk bogging things down. One way or another, though, find out what you need to know. If you do, you'll be genuinely knowledgeable about things and running up to speed in no time.

2. *Look forward to your* next *career.* Does this sound premature? Maybe, but time marches on. Because we can no longer count on security in today's workworld, we've got to be ever vigilant, growing, evolving. Why wait until someone X'es you off a list and you suddenly lose a great job you worked so hard to get? Instead, keep your career life vibrant, prosperous, meaningful, and even fun.

    The other incentive for thinking about your next position *now* is that all of us change over time. What may have meant everything to us five years ago may mean nothing at all to us today. Continuing your dream career advancement campaign allows you to live robustly and happily. So keep your career conversations and your career dreams flowing!

Dream Career Advancement Checklist

Using the checklist below, note how many dream career advancement items you've remembered to attend to since getting hired for this new position. If you find any items you can't answer with a simple check for yes, then you've identified some work still ahead of you. But don't wait too long to get going on them. Time, as I just mentioned, marches on.

I've notified all my career allies of my new position. In my notification I've thanked them sincerely for all their assistance and good wishes.

Since starting my new job, I've added many new names to my career allies list.

I've joined a professional organization that represents my new position.

I've volunteered for a committee in my professional organization. I plan to stay very active.

I've begun subscribing to at least two professional magazines relevant to my new position.

I've begun looking for a new mentor. I have approached my new boss about the idea.

I've revised my dream career vision and worked out a timetable for achieving my *next* dream career direction.

SETTLING INTO NEW DIGS

I've set dream goals for my personal life. I have also set down a timetable for achieving these goals.

I've redoubled my efforts to acknowledge
myself for my talents, skills, and achievements.
I reward myself for my courage and determination
every day.

Did You Make a Mistake?

We all make mistakes. Sometimes we even make a whopper. And sometimes, despite all the hard work and careful planning we have done, we realize we have made a mistake by taking this new job. Yet we often can't realize it until it's too late!

So consider this: What would you do if after, say, a couple of weeks at your new job, you begin to feel it isn't right for you, that accepting it has been a big, big error? In such a predicament, the first questions to ask yourself would be: "Do I miss my previous job? Was I happier there? Was my idea of leaving my last career just a case of the grass looking greener somewhere else?"

Depending on your answers to these questions and the way you feel about them, the problem could be that you've chosen the wrong company, the wrong department, or even the wrong career. Maybe you need to rethink your dream career direction. You may simply be still in process, still looking for that dream career direction that's right for you.

The first thing to remember is: Don't panic! You can handle this. You can get yourself to a new place. You know you can do this because, quite simply, you just did it!

Second thing to remember: It's OK to leave. If you want to quit, and if you can afford to, just do it. Give your two weeks notice, take a hike—get out of there! Do what you need to do, for *you*. Set yourself free.

If you have learned anything at all during this dream career process, it should be that you've got to look out for #1, i.e., Y-O-U. Also, you're a very powerful professional who has proved to the world you don't have to stay locked up in a dead-end job or school or unemployment dungeon.

SETTLING INTO NEW DIGS

You have found out about lots of new career possibilities, and you have eased yourself down the road to one of them on the list. You're a winner now, even if your battles are still not over. You have proven you have what it takes.

So go back to good old Square One. Yes, that's right, go all the way back but do not pass GO, and please, please: do not accept $200. **NOTE TO MILLENNIALS:** I'm referring to a 20th Century game called Monopoly, which you possibly have never played! Way different from Game of Thrones.

However, it's not *really* Square One, of course, it's at least Square Two, or Square Three, or perhaps even Square Four. Remember, you're not starting out as a naïve greenhorn this time. So inhale deeply and believe that the next DCD will be the one you really want. Then start thinking about which one that will be.

Legion of Career Heroes

KATHY OPAL GOFF: M.D.

In her mid-thirties, Kathy O. Goff (Opal) had been a very successful engineer, well on her way to higher levels of professional stature and responsibility. When she came to us at CareerScape, she had been working for a major scientific research firm near Boston, reaping the benefits of all that this enviable situation entailed: good salary, good benefits, home ownership, secure job. Yet something had started to eat away at her, something on the level of: "Is this it? Is this all there is?"

While pondering what else she might do instead, and even wondering if she had a right to so much as think about something "instead," she recalled that she had always wanted to be a doctor when she was growing up. Her wish to become a doctor, however, got put aside as she grew older and began to face her career-setting decision of choosing a college major. She had a very high ideal of what doctors should be like and didn't think she could live up to that ideal. She didn't think to discuss this with parents, teachers, or advisors. She convinced herself that becoming an engineer might be more practical than studying medicine. So she let herself be steered toward engineering, earned her degree in that field, won a job at a good company right out of school, then applied herself for over a decade to be the best engineer she could be.

But now here she was realizing that, if she was being truly honest with herself, she had always wanted to be a doctor. And, scary though that thought might be, she was sure she could accomplish it if she decided to give it a try. Though she was older than the typical med student, it was neither too late nor impractical. And she now knew she already had many of the people skills that good doctors need; the same ones that, as a teen, she had thought she lacked. Since she was not yet tied down with

SETTLING INTO NEW DIGS

a family, she really was free as a bird to pursue her dream. It would be tough and challenging yes ... but possible.

Opal's career conversations evolved into seeking out doctors to "shadow" to test how the idea felt. This shadowing went well enough for her to begin studying for her medical boards. During the summer months of that year, she dragged her old chemistry textbook and other related materials to the beach and re-familiarized herself with their pages. Then in the fall she took the boards and passed. "At that point," she laughs now, "there was no turning back!"

Next came acceptance into medical school, with financing arranged through loans, savings and the selling of her house. A few years later, she joined a family medicine practice and engineering became a thing of her past. With a special focus on the whole patient and a particular emphasis on communicating clearly, compassionately and effectively with her patients[*], Dr. Kathy Opal Goff both discovered and achieved her lifelong dream career.

---

[*] not to mention a passion for encouraging them to seek fulfilling careers

11

THOUGHTLEADING FOR CAREER SUCCESS

Beyond all my (ahem!) obviously brilliant and wise information and advice in this book, the smartest dream career explorers will heed and implement the contents and message of this very special chapter. Here is where I suggest you go way, way, way beyond thinking of yourself as a career switcher, college grad out for your first job, unemployed job seeker, professional re-entering the workforce etc. Instead pursue the status and behavior of an expert with an edge, a guru if you will, or, as I like to term it, a "thought leader."

If you are willing to embrace the concept of yourself-as-a-business, which is what you are of course, you need to also embrace marketing and selling techniques, and not just *any* marketing and selling techniques but *superior* marketing and selling techniques. That requires you to position yourself as a thought leader.

What exactly do I mean by that? And why would I suppose you could easily become one?

In a nutshell, a thought leader is an expert whom people view as such. Though everyone with a job of any kind could rightly be labeled an "expert" … including your favorite barista down at Starbucks or that guy you saw slipping down a manhole this afternoon, and into the sewer tunnel, to take care of … ah … to handle some … oh … to, ah … well heck I don't know *what* he's doing down there! And that in fact is how we know he's an expert, because he is knowledgeable about a work or professional area that we are not. That makes him an expert.

But is he a thought leader or guru or expert with an edge? Is he someone to whom people would immediately think to seek out whenever they might need help in the particular way that he can provide? In most cases, the answer would be negative. After all most professionals are capable of being viewed as experts with an edge over their colleagues or competition, i.e., "thoughtleaders" (I now hereby squeeze these two words together into ONE word) but since no one knows about them, they fail to win the big thoughtleader prize!

So the key is to get this message out, to create high-level visibility, to become "famous" on some level, maybe not mega-famous but famous nonetheless on a local level or within a niche. In that way, a part of the world views you as an expert who is a cut above the rest, i.e., a guru or thoughtleader.

So next I'll explain how you can join these ranks of high-caliber experts and thoughtleading gurus, but before I do let's be very clear about why you should. Thoughtleaders are sought out, people look for them, they're ready to hire them, pay them money. Yes, that seems to have gotten your attention, right? Dozing off there a bit for a moment?

And yes if it works for businesses, why shouldn't it also work for employers seeking outstanding employees to hire? Thus, rather than competing with the masses for hyper-advertised job slots, what if instead you started to find yourself courted by employers who came looking for you (not the other way around) and then told you they wanted you and only you for such-and-such a position... no competition, only *you*!

Or, alternatively, how about if you found yourself with a few extra dazzling tools in your repertoire that pushed you above all the rest and offered you the capacity to blow away your competition! Yes, yes, yes: blow ... them ... away. Ah, wouldn't that be sweet?

So let's turn now to four thoughtleading tactics that can get you to this dream career nirvana. Try them out, experiment, get good at them, and achieve them. Once you do, most likely you will be the only applicant seriously considered for virtually any job that you choose to pursue:

1. **CARRY "CAREER VALUE" business cards**. Print up some business cards with your name, email, phone and social media info on them, as well as your special expertise, i.e., your "career value." Are you looking for a job in sales, for example? If so, put the phrase "Sales Expert" under your name. Are you a former human resources manager and want to get back in the game? "Human Resources Specialist" fits nicely right there below your name. How about "Wastewater Specialist"? Looks great below your given moniker.

    By thinking like a business, you can use a career value card to display that sophisticated expertise you have worked so hard to attain. Your career value in the marketplace is what will eventually get you your next job, right? So use this simple technique to make everyone that you meet immediately aware of it.

2. **STAY CONNECTED to your contacts via eblasts.** When networking and trading business cards, do not simply go home afterward and toss all these freshly collected cards into a box or a corner. Instead, put them to use!

First send a "nice-to-meet-you" email to each new contact later that day or the very next day, telling them you'll be putting their info on your e-list and social media and inviting them to do the same with your info. Then send out periodic though brief updates of your job search, informing people (your career allies of course!) what you've been learning lately about your targeted career including areas you find most fascinating, areas you have discarded (blech and yech, no longer interested!) and what trends in your career or industry that you've discovered are fascinating, and (finally) what kind of networking leads you'd love someone to send you.

Over time, staying connected via such eblasts will allow your connections to fall into productive categories, such as those who are good at actually referring job leads to you, those who tend to refer new (and good) contacts to you, those who alert you to conferences and helpful networking events etc. Though not everyone on your list will help, many will, and frequently it will be those whom you did *not* expect to do so. But without such a means of staying connected over time, your career allies will wither and fade away. No one you have met will quite know how to help you or what kind of help you really need… or in fact whether you still need any kind of help at all! If they don't hear from you, many will assume (if they still think about you at all) that they are not hearing from you because, of course, you finally landed a job… so you no longer need their help!

3. **PUBLISH your ideas!** I'm not especially talking about publishing your ideas in a blog here, although that's probably better than nothing. The problem with a blog is that everyone has done it or is doing it and there's no special "third-party" credibility, just you doing your thing, whatever it is, at whatever level of quality it is. No extra effort called for here.

But when you get your ideas published in a magazine, journal, newspaper, online e-letter, someone else's website, even someone else's blog, your level of credibility ramps right up because someone besides you (a "third party") has to agree with you that your ideas and writing clarity are worth *their* investing in. It's either slightly harder to do or much, much, much harder to do, e.g., Harvard Business Review, the Wall Street Journal or Fast Company Magazine.

In terms of a book on the other hand, even a self-published book is impressive as all get-out because how many other individual job seekers in the history of this interviewer's life might we guess have ever walked in, shaken hands and said hello, then handed said interviewer a "present" in the form of the interviewee's very own book? Trust me, it has *never* happened!

So if you can pull this one off, you are automatically, immediately, waaaaaay ahead of your competition, no matter who it is.

On the same token, to be able to show off a slick reprint of an article you have written and had published is to push your way up to the top of the list of candidates for this job. The biggest consideration for such a show-and-tell, book or article, however is this: be sure your published work relates directly to the job at hand. If you're interviewing for an accountant position, don't bring along an article you wrote on gardening. If you're interviewing to be hired as a sous-chef, no one wants to see your science fiction novel. Or if you're being considered for an opening as a movie production assistant, it won't help much if you hand your interviewer that insightful article you published on astronomy.

With a properly related topic, however, a book or article reprint is worth its weight in pure gold. You'll establish instant and unexpected credibility, and you will show yourself to be an achiever far beyond the norm, not to mention an expert-with-an-edge, a guru in the very field you're vying for, and a thoughtleader who obviously can handle this particular job, and handle it well. Publishing your ideas clearly proves you've got the right stuff.

NOTE: To learn the process of getting an article or book published, consult my book *The Expert's Edge: Become the Go-To Authority People Turn To Every Time,* published by McGraw-Hill.

4. **SPEAK to professional and community groups.** What professional group out there represents your expertise? Whether in high-tech, finance, management, marketing or whatever, there'll be one or more professional groups that serve you and your colleagues. Google around for the names of these groups, then drop in on a meeting. Ultimately you want to join them as a new member and volunteer to help them out. That way you'll end up making great contacts, getting genuine help with your career, experiencing great speakers, and attending conferences where you'll learn a lot about this profession and where you'll meet well-heeled and well-established professionals. Perhaps

too you'll do some writing for the group's publication (see #3 above!) and you'll speak at one or more of its events. And remember, everyone you meet gets added to your burgeoning e-list (#2 above!).

Speaking is a lot like publishing, it gets your name out there, it gets you out there and it establishes you firmly as a guru, an expert-with-an-edge and a thoughtleader. Once people start seeing you up there on a platform teaching them about an area of your profession that they themselves may not know as much about as they'd like, you'll be well set up for employers to come seeking you out and offering a position they have been wondering how they might fill. Hand out reprints of your latest published article to everyone in the audience and you'll have it made!

Heed these four little-used thoughtleading techniques and you will easily separate yourself from even job competitors who, at first glance, appear much more qualified than you do. Instead *you* will be the one getting noticed, not them. They'll have a cover letter and resume and not much more. But you will have positioned yourself as someone really special, beyond the pale, and someone to watch (and hire).

NOTE TO ENTREPRENEURS: If your DCD seems to be pointing you toward a life of true entrepreneurialism, e.g., your own consulting firm, law or medical practice, retail operation, franchise etc., these thoughtleading techniques will prove invaluable. They represent the crux of effective branding and marketing and will catapult you to the top of the heap even during your business's early stages of growth. So pay attention!

Composing Your "Impact Message"

When a program host invites audience attendees to stand up and give their "30-second elevator speech," you should jump right up and be the first to go. Not only will you be grabbing an unexpected chance to practice, but what you say in those 30 seconds may put you as much in the spotlight as the keynote speaker.

For example, I call my elevator speech an "impact message" and have relationship capital expert Jim Masciarelli to thank for it as Jim is the thoughtleader who designed it.

My impact message typically grabs great attention for me from an audience because it hits them squarely where they live. My impact message follows Masciarelli's careful construction as described in his book *PowerSkills*:

"Hello, my name is Ken Lizotte, I'm with emerson consulting group in Concord Massachusetts," I begin, then after a momentary pause (for effect), I say, "where I make consultants famous!"

"I do this by helping them get their ideas published, thereby positioning them as thoughtleaders and go-to authorities in their field.

"If you'd like to gain more recognition in your target market as an expert with an edge, see me tonight so we can exchange business cards and emails.

"Again I'm Ken Lizotte, emerson consulting group, Concord Massachusetts."

Then I sit down while many in the room murmur and plan to approach me later to exchange business cards. Gets 'em every time!

How to Construct Your Own

THE ATTENTION GRABBER: Hello my name is _____ (add company name and location and/or website) of _____ at _____ and I (catchy value proposition here)_____

THE EXPLANATION: I do this by (specific deliverable)_____, (more than one is acceptable but not more than four… and keep each one brief!)

THE RESULT: … thereby (specific action and/or outcome) _____ _____

SUGGEST WHAT THEY MIGHT GAIN FROM YOU: So if you'd like to gain/get/learn to …

_____, come see me at the break or after the program so we can exchange business cards.

REPEAT: name, company name, location and/or website

NOTE: To learn more about employing a "thoughtleading strategy" as well as other business-savvy attention-getting techniques, consult my book *The Expert's Edge: Become the Go-To Authority People Turn To Every Time*, published by McGraw-Hill, or visit my website www.thoughtleading.com

12

UPON GRADUATING FROM COLLEGE

By the time you're about to graduate from college, or grad school, if you have begun to employ any of this book's techniques you'll be well on your way to fielding job offers and quite possibly even have a solid first-job position already nailed down and waiting for you.

How can I say that in such never-ending times of job stress and intense competition? Simple: focusing on your actual passion vs. so-called "practical" job goals will put you far ahead of the game. No vehicle illustrates this better than the career education option known as internships.

At my own firm, for example, I have frequently conducted a summer internship program for those who might like to learn about writing, editing, publishing, business and consulting. Over 9 weeks starting the first week in June and typically ending the first week in August, we teach all of these topics including hands-on practice for our interns and field trips and conference calls that bring them into contact with editors, publishers, writers, CEOs and consultants and business experts of all stripes.

The first summer I conducted this program, I assumed that each intern would be experiencing a one-time business educational process that, upon completion, might help her or him identify where to go next in choosing a major and/or a minor, what next to explore in terms of career conversations in certain fields, what jobs to begin applying to, what career to ultimately settle into. And all of those results did occur.

However in December of that year, I got a voice message that evolved my thinking. In addition to these genuinely healthy results for my internship graduates, I learned that I as an employer could benefit on a higher level as well. That's because that voice message was from a Gap retail manager who had me down as a reference for an applicant for holiday season work who had once "worked" for me.

Naturally, I gave college student Stacy an excellent reference in such areas as competence, industriousness, quick thinking, quick learning, customer service skills and all the rest, but in doing so I suddenly realized that I had trained Stacy to perform duties on the same highly competent level at my own firm, and that, although I could not afford to pay her a lucrative professional salary for her efforts, I could certainly afford to pay a higher hourly wage than the Gap was offering, i.e., minimum wage.

So I contacted Stacy and told her that, if she wanted, she could come in to work for me during the holiday season too, and that I would pay her for doing so. She appreciated the invitation, never dreaming that there might be such an opportunity, and so for the next few weeks, I had a well-trained operative who loved the professional-level work I could provide for her, and who, despite her relative inexperience compared to professionals who had been doing the same work for many years previously, did just as good a job for me and in some ways better, because she was totally in synch with what my business processes and goals were all about.

This brainstorm on my part led me to prefer hiring college students who had "graduated" from my summer internship vs. my poring over stacks of boring resumes and enduring face-to-face interviews with masses of unfamiliar applicants, no matter how qualified they might be. By now I had come to know (and like) the individuals who had met the learning challenges of my summer programs and thus much preferred continuing working side-by-side with any one of them day to day as opposed to relative strangers.

So over the ensuing years I hired such brilliant permanent staffers as Michaela St. Onge upon her graduation from Lafayette College, Lauren Fleming just after her receiving her diploma from Fordham, and Elena Petricone, an alumna of Hampshire College. All have proven equal to the professional task, not to mention contributing positive and collaborative energy to my firm's mission and client interactions. That someone else out there might have done a *better* job than Michaela, Lauren or Elena has never ever crossed my mind.

An Internship Just for You

Don't look to apply only to *formal* internship programs either. Your search for internships should initially lead you to websites of companies you would LOVE to work for, many of which will be advertising for interns and posting info on their upcoming internship programs (including dates, qualifications needed, other requirements etc.). And of course there are internship listing and matching services that can introduce you to internship programs you would otherwise never have known existed.

But consider too offering yourself as an intern to organizations that may not even have a formal program in place, especially if they are a place you're personally drawn to. Ask around too (via your career eblasts, for example) about internships that your career allies might know about but which, again, you might otherwise not know about or be able to locate via standard research. I suggest this line of thinking from another experience of mine in the area of taking on interns.

Now and then an intern has come to me out of the blue, typically not because they had happened upon my website's internship section or an internship posting I had placed on a matching service but instead because they simply set out to find an internship like mine. So in both cases they emailed people they knew, in my case in the PR or media fields, basically fishing for any ideas that might be out there. Via forwarding of their emails to this one and then that one, all of a sudden, in both cases, they ended up in my inbox. Though the professional folks that preceded me neither offered, nor had any interest in offering, any kind of internship opportunity, I of course did.

So in both cases, I responded to these emails to say that I wanted to learn more about them and that, yes, possibly, I could take them on as an intern. This would mean a different arrangement from my summer June-August program organized for college students because in both of these out-of-the-ordinary cases, I was now dealing with individuals who were either working at a totally different full-time job (Precious Kirk, flight attendant) or coming off a related internship in her native country (Aurelie Hiernaux, Belgium). Both had emerged during the winter as well so waiting until the summer was not what they were looking for.

Long story short, I went back and forth with each of them, learning about them and their goals and answering their questions about my company's services and *its* goals, coming to a meeting of the minds so that I was willing to set up an individual internship program for them both. The outcome was beneficial to all concerned, despite the fact that each internship lived outside the bounds of the formal one that I had set up years before.

So do not assume a company or nonprofit that does not list a formal internship program on its website automatically has no interest in offering such. Remember what happened to Rick DeAngelo, volunteering (basically interning) for a gigantic corporation! Each year when I would bring my summer interns to the CEO Club of Boston, of which I am a member, and let them introduce themselves (via their impact message of course!), I would also field questions from my fellow CEOs about how I had come to set up such a program and what advice did I have for them to set up one of their own. Basically, most of them had no clue whatsoever how to go about it nor had they given it much thought.

The takeaway here then is to not hesitate to approach an organization that you would love to learn from and possibly work for one day just because you can't find a formal internship program there to apply to. You never know what might happen if you take a chance and break away from your assumptions.

Keys to the Kingdom

So the keys to the kingdom of career life after college have much to do with your career habits as well as relationships you can initiate before you graduate, in addition to an understanding of how to continue to breed and sustain career relationships after getting thrust out of the warmth of the campus and into that cold, cruel, sordid workworld you have been hearing so much about. But in addition to internships, career conversations and other techniques we have discussed so far, what specifically college resources can you access that your college posse, by and large, will likely have ignored?

Here are a few, off the very top of my bushy head:

Alumni Association: This is the big one, no matter what institution you are studying at; because this represents that one big happy family you've been a part of for nearly four full years. Every college has successful graduates in every career field, all of whom (*all* of whom) will likely be willing to at least do a career conversation with you. So, get on down to the college career office, or alumni office, or wherever, and find out how you can utilize this gold mine.

Career Office: Since you're down there anyway, what else can your college career office offer you? A one-on-one counselor, maybe? Classes in resume-writing and networking and trendy job openings? Special software or online networks for skills evaluation and talents assessment?

Believe it or not, many people assume the college career office has nothing really to offer them and thus never even check it out. That's crazy ... at least check it out! Besides, you've been paying for this service all along with your hefty, outrageous tuition ... or, ah, your parents have!

Faculty: Wondering who else to do career conversations with, i.e., where to find experts in this or that field to collar for a brain-picking good cup of coffee or tea (your treat of course)? How about that older guy or gal right there in front of you every day or at least 2-3 times a week? That's right, you got it ... your professor!

Not only can your screenwriting professor or chemical engineering teacher or business instructor or sociology prof help you understand the course subject matter in a career-beneficial way, he/she also (a) knows a lot of people in the field (not just alumni), (b) has probably had experience off campus with your DCD, (c) can help you understand the pitfalls as well as the joys of your DCD, and (d) can offer helpful advice on your resume draft, impact message, proposed job hunting strategy and potential employers who might offer you the best fit.

Keep these special folks in mind, don't just brush right past them. The homework they give you this time just may result in a job!

On-campus organizations: What have we said so far about professional associations and career gatherings? With so many similar groups right there on campus, why wait until graduation to hone your networking skills and develop relevant career relationships? At least visit once or twice the science club, the pre-med ski club, the young entrepreneurs club, the high-techie intramural Frisbee league, the film society, the economics society or the socially responsible Thursday night ice cream collaborative. You'll not only learn more about your DCD and build new (and potentially powerful) career relationships ... you might even have a little fun!

Visiting speakers: Either independent of the options above or perhaps due to a sponsorship by any one of them, take part as well in visits to your college by off-campus famous and/or highly successful career speakers.

Interested in a career in the arts? Get over tonight to attend a lecture by the curator of a New York or LA or Chicago museum.

Intrigued by a possible job in the sports field? Do not miss the general manager of the local professional hockey team or a famous coach or player from the NBA, Major League Baseball, the NFL or the National Soccer League.

Might politics be your game? Guess who's coming to campus... a high-ranking official in the White House or one of your college's two US Senators, or even perhaps the mayor of the college's hosting town.

In short, scout out and take advantage of resources that are all around you. Your campus is full of them and you can only utilize most of them while you are right there as a full-time student. This too will prove an advantageous skill in the years to come after college because even though resources will be all around you, the sad fact for most people in life, on campus or off, is an inability to recognize this or to employ such resources in pursuit of personal goals.

You of course, my faithful and attention-paying reader, will be different.

UPON GRADUATING FROM COLLEGE

Legion of Career Heroes
MY BROTHER ED: Part-time to Full-time

Never pass up an opportunity to leverage part-time work or temporary work or a freelance project or summer work (even while still in school) toward a full-time, permanent dream career position. Maybe you're a temp worker for example and you do such good work that the company which had felt it needed someone like you "for only a short time" has now decided it cannot survive without you. They ask the temp agency if they can hire you away from them and change your status from temporary to indefinitely, i.e., permanent.

My brother Ed Lizotte achieved something like this by parlaying a part-time job in high school at the supermarket chain Stop & Shop into his first professional dream career position six years later. Though a mere retail clerk during those high school years in Massachusetts, when he went off to study at Fairfield University in Connecticut, he asked to be transferred to a Stop & Shop near the college where he worked nights and weekends during all four years.

Approaching graduation when he would be awarded a degree in finance, he used his Stop & Shop network to arrange an interview with the company's MediMart division, a CVS-type chain of drugstores. The combination of his college degree, years of service to Stop & Shop and obvious good personal fit with the opening led to an entry-level position in MediMart's accounting department.

Thus years of stocking shelves and hauling cartons of canned goods had led directly to a terrific professional situation, starting him down a dream career path that led to a position as a company controller with a major manufacturer and ultimately the successful financial advisor practice that 27 years later he still conducts today.

13

RETIREMENT IS NOT AN OPTION

What's important now about retirement is that it doesn't have to be, at least not in the sad "out-to-pasture" scenario. Granted, some of you may want to put yourselves out to pasture. Or at least out to the greens of your favorite golf courses or the loam-laden environs of your front or backyard's personal gardens. Maybe playing with your grandchildren, volunteering for a few local organizations, bagging groceries part-time at the local super mart and/or reading a lot more than you ever could during your working life while hanging out with genial regulars at bingo is enough for you. Maybe you've just plain had enough of work, work hours, work responsibilities, work challenges, work frustrations and work dress codes so that now, well, you are happy to finally be able to take a breather. If so, good for you... take it!

However, for some of us, retirement of that sort will never be enough. For us, we may want to cut back a bit and not be so time-consumed or cutthroat or ambitious or filled with anxiety ... *but* ... just running away from it all is simply not a satisfactory answer. Instead, call them bucket lists or new ventures or challenges at this next phase of life, whatever you like, we've got to tackle *something*. So look forward to your retirement years not with fears that can't be tamed but with creative notions of what you might achieve. Life's not over... so why stop?

Some years ago, when John Kenneth Galbraith was still around, at the age of 87 in fact (he eventually passed away ten years later at the age of 97), a Boston Globe op-ed of his explored use of the word "still" in relation to his current aging status. "People ask me these days things like 'Are you still writing?' or 'Are you still doing public speaking?'" he wrote. "Why must the word 'still' be injected into the question? Why would I NOT be doing these things that I have always done? Why would I stop doing them? And if I did... what would I do with myself instead?"

The idea that retirement *must* enter our lives and *must* slow us down and *must* even stop us from doing things we have always loved, or that we might love if we finally got a chance to try them, just because we're a certain age, is a relic of a far earlier era when people, as they aged, seemed to automatically get less healthy. The retirement age of 62, for example, was chosen at a time when the median age for death was 65. In the many decades since then, so many health advances have been achieved that now the median age is much, much higher and stories about baby boomers running marathons into their 80s or still taking the bus to their offices past the age of 90+ or writing a book at age 70 or getting elected to office at 69 (Ronald Reagan) or 74 (Jerry Brown) abound. We are just no longer shackled by our health ... by our age maybe but not our age per se because by continuing to eat right, get enough sleep, exercise, eliminate smoking and other risk factors, one could be 90 or 95 or even over 100 and still be fit as a fiddle for a good day's work.

So how can we look for a new job or start a whole new career once we have officially "retired" at age 65 or so? In most respects, it's as simple as paying attention to all the strategic measures identified in this book regardless of chronological age, e.g., career conversations, building career allies, practicing thoughtleading, creatively re-structuring your resume etc. It may seem age discrimination or people's misconceptions of "old age" will work against you but if you aim toward a new DCD and end-run the conventional process of competing with hoards of resumes, you'll likely land in an enviable spot for anyone of any age.

After all, why wouldn't someone want to hire you if you offer more experience, more wisdom, more maturity, more flexibility and more stability than someone way younger? Why wouldn't someone prefer you in a consultant's role to some greenhorn with less accumulated knowledge and fewer lessons learned? Why wouldn't someone want to consider purchasing your new product or service based on a proven formula or solution than a cheaper product or service that's obviously inferior from some young whippersnapper?

The greatest hindrance then to your keeping yourself cranked up and pushing beyond the conventional retirement of 65 or thereabouts may be you and you alone. It's probably in your own mind that you are *supposed* to retire, or that no one would want you, or that you're—gasp!—"over the hill." Quite likely nothing could be further from the truth.

So what may be the best inspiration to get you past all that is a role model that speaks to you in some special or personal way. Yes it may be quite as simple as all that, someone to model, someone whose lead you can follow, someone to prove that it can be done. If he or she could do it, you may need to be feeling ... so can I! To help you out on that score, skim through the following "post-retirement" anecdotes and when you find something you like, latch onto it and get your own creaky, tired bones moving in a similar direction all your own:

Dot Higgins: A schoolteacher throughout her adult life in addition to raising a family, Dot Higgins had always been a civic spirit. Volunteering whenever she could to help out local groups, she made her avocation tendencies a full-time occupation by writing a local events column for her town's weekly newspaper and volunteering to assist such small town endeavors as charity road races, fund-raising events and children's causes. As of this writing, at age 94, she is still going strong.

Dr. Bob Carey: After graduating from Harvard Medical School in the mid-20th Century, Dr. Bob Carey spent the next 56 years practicing medicine, treating patients, advocating for widespread medical care and even founding a special scholarship for medical interns to spend time caring for the rural poor in South America. One day, seeking a means of helping to fund this scholarship program, he took his family's advice and began to write a book *Patients Teach a Doctor About Life and Death: Tales from Fifty-Six Years of Practicing*. He was in his 80s when it was finally published, followed by an aggressive speaking and book promotion campaign.

George Burns: A vaudeville star in his early years, George went on to great success as a radio star, then TV star with his comedienne wife Gracie Allen, whom he always lauded as the smarter and funnier half of their act. After she died of a heart attack at the age of 69, George had to decide whether to continue with show business or hang it up and retire for a well-deserved rest. He chose to continue because, he used to say, "I can rest when I die." By his mid-90s he had a particular goal: to do his stand-up act at Caesars Palace at age 100. Caesars jumped at the idea and signed him up for a run of performances in the year 1996. Alas, however, George didn't make it, passing at age 100 mere weeks before the gig was to start. One assumes that in that great Caesars Palace in the sky, George ultimately did go on, spinning out his well-honed shtick, this time with Gracie once again at his side co-telling a few final jokes.

Satchell Paige: Satch had been a fearsome pitcher in the old Negro Baseball League until Jackie Robinson paved the way for him to be acquired by the Cleveland Indians in 1948 when he became, at age 42, the oldest rookie ever to play Major League Baseball. He stayed on for many more years racking up respectable statistics and even being named to two All-Star games and eventually the Baseball Hall of Fame. He pitched his last game in the majors in 1965. His autobiography "Don't Look Back" was a play on a personal motto "Don't look back, something might be gaining on ya." Yet another of his life philosophies may have said it even better: "It's just mind over matter … if you don't mind, then it don't matter."

Kentucky Colonel Harland Sanders, the founder of Kentucky Fried Chicken, was well into his 60s before KFC really took off as a lucrative franchised operation. Previously he had been a successful but small local service station owner who also sold food. Until his death at age 90, he would travel as many as 250,000 miles per year across the globe to visit his far-flung fried chicken empire.

Jack LaLanne: Jack was always a successful bodybuilder, personal trainer, TV exercise guru, inventor of the leg extender still used in gyms today and self-acclaimed "health nut." By the time he was 70, however, he wanted to really show people how getting older did not necessarily mean getting frail. So well into his 70s, he demonstrated such physical feats as: swimming while handcuffed from Alcatraz to San Francisco, pulling (also while swimming) 70 boats (yes, handcuffed this time too), and founding and marketing a successful juicer business at the age of 88, for which he did numerous infomercials with his wife Elaine, until his demise at the age of 96.

Jack Borden: As reported by the Wall Street Journal a few years back, "When Jack Borden was 60, he still had at least 40 more years of work in front of him. And now, at 101, the Weatherford, Texas lawyer seems determined to put in a few more … he still dons a coat and tie every weekday and heads down to his law office, where he puts in a full day's work as a probate and real-estate lawyer. Part of (Borden's) ambition stems from the fact, it seems, that his work is keeping him alive. 'If I were to go home and sit down, I wouldn't live another year,' he said. 'I come down here' — to this office — 'really to live.'"

Betty White: We all know her, she's been around with us for such a long, long time, making us laugh in TV sitcoms like "The Mary Tyler Moore Show," "The Golden Girls" and "Hot in Cleveland" (to name only a few) as well as, for some of us, cutting up with her own version of Lucy in a 15-minute daily sitcom in the early Fifties called "Life With Elizabeth." At this writing she is now pushing past 93 and still working such day jobs (plus appearing everywhere she is asked as well). Always leave 'em laughing, as the Catskills comics used to say. Betty White is still doing so.

14

BALANCING WORK AND PERSONAL

People truly achieve balance only when they choose to live the way they want. They feel in balance when they sense centeredness, when they're inwardly confident about what they're doing. Each of us is a unique combination of emotions, thoughts, ideas, abilities, memories, desires. What balances one of us won't necessarily balance the other. I love classical music, you love good old rock and roll. I love Peach Melba, you adore strawberry rhubarb pie. I relax by reading *Scientific American*, you by competing in Monster Tractor Trailer Rallies.

Setting Your Own Standards

Although this seems obvious—that we're all so different—we often spend our lives reaching for someone else's brass ring or trying to emulate a lifestyle that seems as if it should be fulfilling, yet never quite satisfies us. For example:

- The attorney who hates law but couldn't bear to disappoint his lawyer-father and lawyer-grandfather by dropping his practice. He certainly couldn't tell them that he longed instead to be a pro golfer!

- The mother of six who feels she doesn't really work for a living. Although her husband supports her in her choice to stay home and raise their family, she compares herself constantly to working women she sees on talk shows who boast about "having it all."
- The twenty-something single professional who worries about her one-dimensional life. Although she loves her work, loves the travel it demands, and loves the satisfaction of a project well done, she quietly berates herself for socializing more, not finding a mate, not getting married, not settling down and raising a family. Simply working hard and loving it isn't good enough.
- The married couple who so love spending time with each other that they don't seem to want any children. Yet both their mothers keep pushing the question: "Sooo… when are you going to make me a grandmother? Hmmm?" The couple keeps asking each other what's wrong with them.

Did you see yourself in any of these scenarios? Or perhaps you've got one of your own! If you want to define the balance in your life that's right for you, you must first take one critical and difficult step: *Stop listening to everybody but yourself!* You will create true balance in your life only by setting your own standards and fashioning your own definition of balance. You need to decide what personally makes you feel that life is worthwhile.

Need some examples? Here are a few Personal Balance Statements from people I've known to get you thinking about how to define your own. Remember, these are other people's definitions of balance, not yours. They might appeal to you or inspire you, but you will still want to fashion one that's unique to you.

Personal Balance Statements

My vision of a balanced life is one in which I have a few really good friends, not a large entourage.

My vision of personal balance is to work part-time and take care of my family the rest of the time.

I want a life in which I have lots of friends, do lots of socializing, and am busy all the time.

Give me a life that permits me to grow: plenty of reading, thinking, intellectualizing with colleagues!

I envision a life in which I achieve great things in my work but also maintain a happy and loving family life.

A Personal Balance Statement can be very simple, or it can be more complicated with two or more ideas sewn together. I suggest, though, that you keep your Personal Balance Statement fairly simple, at least at first. Your Personal Balance Statement should frame your life, not outline it in detail. Details are the goals, directions, specific steps that you need to take to achieve your Personal Balance. The vision itself must be flexible enough to allow for surprises, obstacles, and opportunities along the way.

Your Personal Balance

Let's try now to define your Personal Balance. If you have trouble, don't worry: we'll be engaging in other exercises to help flesh it out. You can always come back and revise or replace your Personal Balance Statement at any time. Right now we just want to see what comes up spontaneously in a preliminary self-examination.

Start with "I want a life in which . . ." or "My definition of Personal Balance is to..." Use a sheet of poster paper for your Personal Balance Statement. If you have trouble putting it into words, use as much paper as you like to sketch out your feelings or doodle some kind of illustration of what you feel. Exercises throughout this chapter will help you flesh out the definition of your Personal Balance further. **NOTE:** I suggest that, to realize the full impact of this exercise and some of the others in this chapter, you pick up a package of magic markers or borrow a few of your children's crayons (just a few: your kids will need them too!). By using color you'll access more segments of your brain and thus more aspects of yourself. This could result in a truer, more rounded picture of who you are.

Personal Balance Statement

Now let's get a little more specific about what would make your life more balanced. On your poster paper, allow yourself to further imagine, speculate, fantasize, dream. Put down anything you can think of that would make your life fulfilling, worthwhile, exhilarating, or fun. Just fill up the poster paper and keep listing things until you can't think of anything more. Do not censor yourself! This is your chance to get really close to the heart of your Personal Balance Statement.

Think of your ideas as personal aspirations, i.e., "wants" in your life including goals and ambitions from all categories: career, family, friends, social life, spiritual growth, recreation, health. Maybe you can think of other categories too. Your mission here is to flesh out your Personal Balance Statement by getting more detailed about how you want your life to really be.

BALANCING WORK AND PERSONAL

Have you completed your Personal Balance brainstorming? Great! Now sketch out a "Priority Pie Chart" below. Illustrate in this pie chart your ideal of a balanced lifestyle by carving out wedges proportional to the priority you place upon each category of your life. Once again, wedges may include career, family, friends, recreation, spiritual growth, health, and whatever other categories you like. Include sub items in each wedge that elaborate upon each priority. Example: Sub items for "Many good friends" might include "trusting, fun-loving, great dancers, movie-lovers, parties once a month, spontaneous."

Now compare your priorities with the way you currently direct your efforts and time. What do you need to work on to make your present life more consistent with your priorities? Make a list of action steps in the blank space below that you will take to get yourself closer to a balanced lifestyle.

Now you revise or replace your Personal Balance Statement as your Priority Pie Chart implies. What elements did you originally include because you thought you should? What elements did you leave out because you hadn't considered how much they really mean to you? Once you have finished, draw up a revised Personal Balance Statement on a new sheet of poster paper. Remember, flexibility will be your ally throughout this process. If you allow yourself to keep rethinking how to best define your Personal Balance, you will keep it fresh and vibrant, and strong enough to overcome obstacles and changing conditions.

Five Zany Ideas for Living Life to the Nth Degree

We often forget or ignore our capacity to enhance our lives just by thinking and acting differently. We focus on worst-case scenarios and pessimistic projections. Yet some people insist that 90 percent of what we worry about never comes true anyway, so what are we trying to prove? If you're ready, then, to let go of negative airs that keep balance outside the door, try on a few zany, daffy insights that might actually welcome balance in.

1. The World Is Out to Help You!

Ever find yourself believing the opposite, that the world is out to get you? That's pretty easy to do, especially when Murphy's Law seems something like the Magna Carta. Some humor experts advise practicing "random acts of kindness." (You've seen the bumper sticker, perhaps?) Especially in the workplace, they say, kindness and helpfulness generate good vibrations that keep the atmosphere charged with plenty of positive, optimistic energy for all.

Specific suggestions: Stick a happy-face emoticon in a Word doc that your assistant has been proofreading for you. When she gets to that page, say, the middle or so, she'll appreciate the gesture! You can also show appreciation by sending a funny greeting card to colleagues or your supervisor, putting an inspirational saying on the company bulletin board, bringing along a banana pen or a quill to sign important documents at meetings. Just have some fun, for heaven's sakes!

The ice cream maker Ben and Jerry's, for example, offers its workers the opportunity to participate in the company "Joy Gang," an employee committee whose purpose is to spread joy and merriment to all company departments and stores.

Why not start your own joy gang?

2. Take a Break, Why Don't Ya?

Recent brain research indicates that taking mental and physical breaks from extended work periods refreshes people, helps them work out vexing problems, and gets them into a more productive frame of mind when they resume their concentration. Take breaks frequently! Don't be afraid people will think you're slacking off and not working very hard. You'll actually be working *harder*, or at least smarter, by keeping yourself sharp and performing at optimal mental and physical levels.

3. Say "Yes" to Yourself!

You're trying your best, aren't you? You're giving it all you've got, right? Then acknowledge these facts from time to time and give yourself a well-earned pat on the back. It's nice to hear an acknowledgment from someone else, too, of course, but if it doesn't come your way, do something really bold: Ask the other person for it!

One fabulous way to really acknowledge yourself is to give self-rewards from time to time. Did you finish a tough assignment last week? Go out and have that hot fudge sundae you never let yourself indulge in anymore. Forget worrying about eating all those carbs, we're not gonna tell anybody. (In fact . . . I'll join you!)

NOTE OF ADVICE: Make sure you reward yourself not just for your victories, but even for just being you. If you acknowledge only your winning performances, you lose the opportunity to access the self-reward system at times when you may need it most. Keep up your spirits and your self-esteem any way you can. You're human. Say "Yes!" to yourself!

BALANCING WORK AND PERSONAL

4. Program Your Brain Cells for Success!

A time-honored "positive thinking" technique for maintaining a positive attitude is the affirmation card. Write on an index card a statement of something you want, putting this statement in the form of a declarative sentence in the present tense with active verbs. Add superlative adjectives or adverbs.

Example: "I am exceeding my sales quotas every week with great gusto." Or: "I inspire my project team to excellent performances month after month." Or: "I am taking care of all my errands on weekends promptly and efficiently." Whatever you're after, say it in the most winning way.

Is this only some kookie New Age razzle-dazzle that sounds really nice and delicious but doesn't fit the real world? Uh-uh. You can actually program your brain with such simple techniques. Your brain gradually adopts each statement as truth, instructing your thinking processes to matter-of-factly find ways to implement them.

Carry your index cards around with you and read from them about fifteen to twenty times a day. Make out a card for every goal or desire you can think of. This simple, crazy idea really works! After a while, you won't be able to imagine doing things any other way than how you've put them on the card.

5. Connect with Nature!

When you work (and live) so much indoors, it's easy to forget that a key aspect of who you are is your connection with nature. Since we humans have spent most of our millions of developmental years adapting to outdoor environments, it's only natural that true inner balance will be tough to achieve if you don't stay connected to the trees and the breeze.

When you take your breaks, when you acknowledge yourself for who you are, do so as much as possible outside. Find a quiet pond near your home or work, a garden path, an open field or city park, a favorite tree, or a slow country road. Some people swear that without access to a bucolic natural environment they could never ever experience true balance, no matter how powerful are other techniques.

Keep your connection with nature an integral and ongoing segment of your schedule. You've got to have it.

How to Destroy Your Creativity

We all start out curious, creative, determined, and willing. Don't believe us? Look no further than your children (or someone else's). If your eighteen-month-old wants to get closer to the remote control, she'll climb over every obstacle to get to it. She'll clamber over lumbering coffee tables, past teetering floor lamps, around lumpy sofa beds and rickety rocking chairs, and anything else that makes the mistake of sitting squarely in her path.

Once there, she examines every molecule of the mysteriously intricate device she holds now in her tiny hands, and she stays with it until she's figured it out. Or at least until she's bored. Then it's on to the next adventure.

One eye-opening study I read about recently involves a test group of forty-five-year-olds who were measured for their capacities to be creative. Begun in the 1960s, this study found that only 2 percent of this age group could be considered highly creative, according to standards set by the researchers.

So the researchers decided to see what would happen if they moved their experiment down a notch. Testing forty-four-year-olds in exactly the same manner as the forty-five-year-olds, they found once again only 2 percent of the studied group could be entered into their "highly creative" category.

This got experimenters really curious, so they began moving their tests of the age groups downward. They tested forty-three-year-olds. Percentage scoring "highly creative"? Again only 2 percent.

Forty-two-year-olds were tested next. Again, 2 percent. Forty-one-year-olds, then all through the thirties and twenties and teens. Still 2 percent, each and every age group, all the way down.

When the researchers reached children aged seven, however, the percentage scoring "highly creative" finally changed. This time a whopping 10 percent made the grade. At age six, the percentage held at 10 percent, but at age five, inexplicably, the percentage scoring "highly creative" soared greater still … to 92 percent!

What had happened? Why so low for so very long, and then suddenly, at a very, very, very young age, the completely opposite result? What explained the change?

It came to the testers all of a sudden. It was really so very, very obvious. Between the ages of five and eight, children begin attending school!

Thus before we begin traditional learning, before we get funneled into what sometimes amounts to a big social conformity factory, we apparently function as purely creative beings. But what society values and teaches us at school gets reinforced at work and, unfortunately all too often, at home as well. Stagnation bombs, cloaked as realistic and practical tools for living, get lobbed at us all day long. They keep us stuck and stunted, not just personally but organizationally and socially as well.

So watch out for such "stagnation bombs!" You'll know when one hits you by the sinking feeling of dread that spreads immediately into your core. It stops you in your highly creative tracks, rendering you "same as everyone."

You'll recognize stagnation bombs at work by at least one of the following verbal warning signs:

- Forget about it! You're way ahead of your time.
- No one's ever going to buy that. They won't understand.
- We've never done things that way before.
- We're not ready for that.
- Okay, fine. Now let's get back to reality.
- You'll be laughed right out of town with an idea like that.
- We've always done fine without it.
- That's not our problem.
- That's too far-out a change. No one will go for it.
- We've already tried that idea.
- It's a great idea but it'll never work.
- It's a great idea but we could never pull it off in time.
- You're not serious?
- Has anyone else ever tried this? We wouldn't want to be the first!

A Willingness to be Human

Finally, inside all of us lies a generosity and willingness to contribute and have fun that many people feel keep them in balance all their lives. You won't find these qualities on any anatomical chart, and there is no direct proof that they exist, other than lots and lots of anecdotal evidence. But we know they are there.

Your willingness to be human, to touch others in your life, to be open to new experiences, to listen to and respond to others, to learn from everything and everyone, to make those around you laugh: all these qualities are keys to balance. Human touch is contagious and inspires others to live balanced lives even as it affirms and maintains the life of its originator. Why not let that originator be you?

DISCOVER **YOUR DREAM** CAREER

Legion of Career Heroes

JULIE HORGAN: Soloist

Not all dream career stories begin and end with jobs or business lives. Sometimes, to get us where we want to go, we have to drill down deep into our most personal hopes and dreams and FEARS. That can mean pursuing totally non-career goals, if only to redeem ourselves from decisions we once made about pathways not taken. At that point, we may achieve a personal balance that frees us up in such a way we can now, finally, focus on work issues effectively too.

Such was the need for Julie Horgan, who, while musing about potential new career paths, couldn't help dwelling on a personal love that she had never been encouraged to pursue. While little, she had wanted to study music, but adults in her life at the time, e.g., music teachers and her parents, pushed her to give the idea up.

"You don't have any musical talent," they pronounced. "It would be a waste of your time." Julie thus grew up believing this malarkey and let her desire to learn more about music slide away.

When re-evaluating her assumptions about herself at CareerScape however, she found herself resenting what she had accepted as gospel in her younger days. Specifically this took the form of: "Is it true that I really have no talent for music? If that's really true, then why do I still love it so? And how does anybody else know if I could learn a musical instrument, and even get good at it?"

So Julie, at age 41, finally decided to put all that discouragement thrown at her as a kid to the test, by signing up for violin lessons. Like any new endeavor, the first few months of this were hard yet she never considered dropping out. The struggle itself of undertaking music lessons felt exhilarating to her, like she was living a dream.

Within the next year, 40-something Julie found herself participating in a recital with other classmates (some one-fourth her age!) at her music school. Her spectacular achievement that recital day? A solo rendition of "Mary Had a Little Lamb." For all that this gave her, she might as well have been playing Carnegie Hall!

EPILOGUE

A well-known quote from W.H. Murray, the Scottish explorer who trekked through previously untouched regions of the Himalayas, describes a spirit of will you're going to need in order to make the ideas throughout this book come true for you. It goes like this:

> Until one is committed, there is hesitancy, the chance to draw back, always ineffectiveness. Concerning all acts of initiative (and creation) there is one elementary truth, the ignorance of which kills countless ideas and splendid plans: that the moment one definitely commits oneself, then Providence moves too.
>
> All sorts of things occur to help one that would never otherwise have occurred. A whole stream of events issues from the decision, raising in one's favor all manner of unforeseen incidents and meetings and material assistance, which no man could have dreamed would have come this way.
>
> I have learned a deep respect for one of Goethe's couplets: "Whatever you can do, or dream you can, begin it. Boldness has genius, power and magic in it."

That's really the way it is. You can meet this challenge—you really can. You can change your career life; you can escape your current or previous one. You've always been so much more than how you've been defined up to now.

EXPECT **NOTHING**

ACHIEVE **MUCH**

ENJOY **EVERYTHING**

ABOUT THE AUTHOR AND CAREERSCAPE

Ken Lizotte CMC, CIO (Chief Imaginative Officer) of **emerson consulting group inc.**, Concord, Massachusetts, is author of *The Expert's Edge: Become the Go-To Authority People Turn to Every Time* (McGraw-Hill) and four other books. A popular keynoter for such venues as the CEO Club of Boston, the Institute of Management Consultants, Harvard University Extension School, the Association of Management Consulting Firms and the American Management Association, he is also co-founder of the National Writers Union, a Certified Management Consultant, graduate of Alan Weiss's Million Dollar Consulting College and president of Thoreau Farm, the birthplace house of Henry David Thoreau. Ken's been interviewed by the New York Times, Newsweek, Fortune, Business Week, CBS-TV, NPR, Financial Times, Investors' Business Daily, Writer's Digest, and many more.

In 1988, he and his wife Barbara co-founded **CareerScape**, which empowered more than 10,000 professionals to effectively explore and discover a new career direction, i.e., "dream career," at pivotal moments in their lives. CareerScape has been profiled by such major media as the syndicated TV newsweekly Chronicle, the Boston Globe, the Boston Herald, Ladies Home Journal, Boston-area TV stations and radio stations in both the US and Canada.

DISCOVER **YOUR DREAM** CAREER

Sign up for CareerScape's eblasts and receive ongoing tips for career success, notifications of seminars, podcasts and webinars, and articles on various aspects of strategies for business and personal success. To learn more, visit **www.thoughtleading.com/about/careerscape**

Ken and Barbara live in Concord, Massachusetts with their daughter Chloe and their Golden Retriever Chance.

ABOUT EMERSON CONSULTING GROUP INC.

F ounded by Ken Lizotte in 1996, **emerson consulting group inc.** has since transformed literally hundreds of solo business experts and large professional service firms into "thoughtleaders." Its clients include experts in management consulting, IT consulting, financial expertise, legal services, human resources experts, benefits planners, coaching services, and many more, both for-profit and nonprofit.

Emersongroup services are based upon Ken's "five pillars of thoughtleading" as outlined in his book *The Expert's Edge: Become the Go-To Authority People Turn to Every Time,* published by McGraw-Hill. These five pillars comprise a "thoughtleading strategy" designed to position experts and firms as gurus to be recognized by their target markets, thus separating them from the competitive pack.

Ken cites Pillar #1, Publishing Ideas, as the most important of all, due to its impact on all the major business values, such as credibility, branding, visibility & promotion, fresh thinking and expanded expertise, innovation and customer loyalty. Publishing works best when authoring a book and/or articles, especially articles published by third-party media, e.g., journals, e-letters, magazines, newspapers, knowledge websites, guest blogging etc.

Sign up for emersongroup eblasts and receive ongoing tips on publishing and thoughtleading, notifications of seminars, podcasts and webinars, and articles on strategies for business success. To learn more, visit **www.thoughtleading.com**

RESOURCES

The Expert's Edge: Become the Go-To Authority People Turn to Every Time (McGraw-Hill) by Ken Lizotte

Balancing Work and Family (AMACOM Books) by Ken Lizotte and Barbara A. Litwak

Divine Intuition: Your Inner Guide to Purpose, Peace, and Prosperity (Jossey-Bass) by Lynn A. Robinson

A Whack on the Side of the Head: How You Can Be More Creative (Business Plus) by Roger von Oech

Feel the Fear and Do It Anyway (Ballantine Books) by Susan Jeffers

What Color Is Your Parachute? 2015: A Practical Manual for Job-Hunters and Career-Changers (Ten Speed Press) by Richard Bolles

Guerrilla Marketing for Job Hunters 3.0 (Wiley) by Jay Conrad Levinson

Monster Careers: How to Land the Job of Your Life (Penguin) by Doug Hardy (coauthored with Jeff Taylor)

DISCOVER **YOUR DREAM** CAREER

Monster Careers: Interviewing: Master the Moment That Gets You the Job (Penguin) by Doug Hardy (coauthored with Jeff Taylor)

Diary of a Company Man (Globe Pequot Press) by James S. Kunen

Goodbye College – Hello Life! (HRD Press) by Lisa Brock

PowerSkills (Nimbus Press) by Jim Masciarelli

Million Dollar Consulting (McGraw-Hill) by Alan Weiss

Entrepreneurs Inside: Accelerating Business Growth and Corporate Entrepreneurs (Corporate Entrepreneurs LLC) by Susan Foley

Trust Your Gut: How the Power of Intuition Can Grow Your Business (Kaplan Publishing) by Lynn A. Robinson

Paul Falcone is a human resources thoughtleader and speaker who has authored 9 books on critical career issues. Learn more at **www.paulfalconehr.com**

The CareerScape Network: Discover your dream career with the help of a CareerScape-recommended trainer or coach! To learn more, visit **www.thoughtleading.com/about/careerscape**

www.ingramcontent.com/pod-product-compliance
Lightning Source LLC
Chambersburg PA
CBHW071701160426
43195CB00012B/1539